The Royal Horticultural Society

new
classic
gardens

Jill Billington

page 1 A concrete path makes a direct line that is softened by arabesques of bricks set along its length.

page 3 In a design by Steve Martino the stark simplicity of a slate-paved terrace is edged by a sunken trough of reflective water and offset by the wide landscape it overlooks.

this page Modern gardens may be inspired by the past and by other cultures. In this tranquil garden, oriental-influenced raked gravel dominates the centre while a Lutyens seat is set against a plain rendered wall. Self-seeded aquilegias soften the gravel texture.

page 7 The contemporary garden draws from the past as it leads us to a different future. From primitive spiralling earth 'mazes' to sophisticated classical geometry and minimal elegance, there is now an entirely different approach, even to the potager of old, seen here in this formally modern vegetable garden.

To Julia Brett with much appreciation of her friendship, talent and support

Editorial Director: Jane O'Shea
Creative Director: Mary Evans
Art Director: Françoise Dietrich
Project Editor: Carole McGlynn
Design Assistant: Jim Smith
Production: Vincent Smith, Sarah Tucker
Picture Research: Nadine Bazar
Picture Assistant: Sarah Airey

First published in the United States of America by
Rockport Publishers, Inc.
33 Commercial Street
Gloucester, Massachusetts 01930
Telephone (978) 282-9590
Facsimilie (978) 283-2742
www.rockpub.com

First published in 2000 by Quadrille Publishing Limited
Alhambra House
27–31 Charing Cross Road
London WC2H OLS

Cataloguing-in-Publication Data: a catalogue record for this book is available from the British Library.

ISBN 1-56496-784-0
Printed and bound in Singapore

contents

introduction

The past influences our every move, so our ideas of what makes a fine garden are inevitably affected by its rich traditions. Gardeners have held fast to these partly because of an enduring affection for plants and also because, in a rapidly changing world, the garden is the last place where we want to feel challenged. Understandably, therefore, real change has come about gradually but some truly great gardens have recently been made with historic references, bridging the gap between history and today's minimal, architecturally based extremes. Traditional layouts and features are still in evidence, though handled in a gently adapted manner or interpreted with a contemporary twist.

While I share many of today's passionately held views on ecological concerns and the contemporary enthusiasm for wild gardens, meadows and native planting schemes, these are not my concern here. Such an approach, however absorbing, represents only one strand of contemporary garden design and the gardens require considerable maintenance and expertise. Ordered formality is an equally strong basis for many modern gardens and it is an approach that has, and will always, persist. Formality was an integral part of garden design from its early beginnings and in every culture. Today, there is a resurgence of highly organized and carefully planned gardens that are not only beautiful to look at but also well regulated and easy to care for.

But order need not mean conformity and today's gardens are more varied and more individual than at any previous time. Imagination runs freely, international influences are absorbed and reinterpreted, new materials have stimulated experimental ideas and the visual arts have suggested new directions to be explored concerning space, form, texture and colour. The garden is now a personal expression of the owner, a totally unique space, resolving and reflecting its special qualities. The creativity of contemporary garden owners and designers is limitless and bold decisions show them to be unafraid to explore every aspect, to push frontiers and abolish prejudice.

Though significant changes in design principles have certainly come about in the last fifty years, the gardens illustrated in this book have not been chosen for their shock value. They are gardens with atmosphere; gardens that arouse an emotional response; gardens that stir us, inviting us in, altering our mood, calming or exciting us. Each of us will have different favourites and some we may dislike; that is the case with all art. Indeed, some

schemes may be less successful than others but their exploration of new ideas is worth following. Yet innovation, a word often applied to modern gardens, should never matter more than the spirit of the garden. Experiment is exciting but in the end it is the place itself, with its underlying design, that must please. New classics have no need of meaningless gimmicks: the ideas that inform them are merely stepping stones to an ideal.

Modern garden designs can be directly attributable to the inspiration found in the application of materials, both old and new. These materials often help to establish a garden's character and are as important as the paint chosen by an artist. But, however inspirational, materials serve rather than dominate, whereas plants have a greater say in the garden's charisma. They are used, not just to fill in designated borders but as an integrated part of the design: trained to fit the garden's scale, clipped and moulded to define its structure and enclose its space, and offering a sculptural focus or blending subserviently into the boundaries. While horticultural minimalism suits the chic town garden, exotics will add a touch of glamour to a formal structure. But the uniqueness of gardens as an art form is that they are not fixed permanently in time – the seasons and the years will alter their look.

In the freedom that characterizes modern garden thinking, style has an international flavour and ideas come from all cultures. Classical symmetry is not as significant as it was: gardens may be planned with an even stricter, grid-like geometry or we may see gardens of asymmetric plan but geometric layout following the lead given by abstract painters like Piet Mondrian. The oriental approach to scale and space has influenced modern formality, creating a new set of classical rules based on fluid, organic lines in which space balances mass. Ornamentation has been considerably reduced, often replaced by form and texture, and colour is now used to create atmosphere rather than simply decorate.

Despite all the experimental designs taking place today, many of the best modern classic gardens are quietly pleasing, ruled by a different aesthetic, with new materials and modified uses. But the adaptations may be so subtle that the different approach remains 'unseen' until a new generation eventually passes judgement, some decades later. The most lasting changes often occur gradually and, in the end, it may be the gentle adjustments that produce the most beautiful and the most enduring gardens of the era.

Many modern gardens refer to their locale just as strongly as those of the romantic landscape gardens of the eighteenth century. Orchard gardens have existed in Europe for centuries: they started as a simple farming method but their timeless beauty, with their linear layout, allows them to be given a contemporary format. In this French apple orchard, designed by Marc Brown, the trees are sparsely planted in a grid pattern that is emphatically stated by immaculate mowing. The long, wide paths bisect one another, creating large squares for rough grass where wildflowers may flourish. Standard fruit trees are sited at the junctions of the close-mown paths where they do better than they would in rough grass and where the fruit is easily collected. The peaceful atmosphere created here can be emulated for the domestic garden.

In the red desert of Mexico, this garden is just as true to its environment and its time. The culture of low adobe buildings is followed in an implacably modern design by Faith Okuma in the garden's freestanding walls which perfectly suit the spirit of the place. The expanse of the flat plane beyond continues within the confines of the garden but is related to the human scale by simple divisions of space, parallel with the lines of the house. Pierced rectangular blocks separate areas but with the soft, blurred character of adobe. The garden bakes in the sun, the land is dry and dusty but the trees will offer protection when in leaf. Until then their skeletal silver forms relieve the geometry. To cool the view from the house and invite people into the garden space, a water chute emerges from along the large central slab wall to fill the raised pool running parallel with the living space.

part 1 :elements

Gardens that raise the spirits and delight the soul have spaces that are in balance and work to please, and it is particularly important in the formal garden that plants and hard materials should be compatible. In modern classic gardens this has meant retaining all that is good from the past – box hedging and stone flags, for example, have been comfortable associates for two thousand years – as well as welcoming in the new. Some of the familiar respected paving materials are now used in unexpected ways in the contemporary formal garden, while mixing old with new offers a variety of different textures.

Thoughtfully chosen materials can emphasize a layout, whether it is reassuringly geometric or serenely asymmetrical. The geometrically planned layouts from the classical past of Europe and the Near East involved making axial routes, bisecting angles and laying out grid patterns. Such planning is still valid and may be enhanced by the wealth of new materials now available as well as the proven materials of the past. Oriental gardens had equally rigorous 'rules' taken from nature, without the conventions of straight lines and right angles. Modern gardens inspired by the Far East recognize this essentially simple, asymmetric style, ideally suited to modern architecture and chic minimalism, and are well placed to make the most of new flowing materials.

materials

In an arid, stony landscape the rendered wall is painted a glorious chrome yellow, a colour inspired by the surrounding desert plants.

new ways with traditional flooring

The paving materials used for centuries include large stone slabs and small setts, both quarried, and bricks made from local sand. In the past the cheaper option was to quarry locally rather than import superior materials, like travertine marble, over huge distances. While much of ancient Rome, for example, is paved with superb local black basalt, whose natural hexagonal structure sliced well to provide rough, strong paving, modern Jerusalem is built from beautiful local cream limestone that unites new buildings with the old city. Using native building materials for gardens ensured that they related well to the vernacular architecture as well as maintaining the spirit of place.

16

The same approach would be fine today if there were still plenty of affordable local materials from a sustainable source. But this ideal is now rarely an option, though attractive alternatives include floors made from mixed materials or from a simulated version of local stone. A more contemporary approach is to ignore the surroundings and allow the design of the site to be inward-looking, perhaps guided by the style of the existing building or just the desires of the owners. The unity of this type of garden lies within, and the materials chosen for its paving and boundaries may dictate its character. This is increasingly the case in the gardens of today and can give us a very free hand.

stone

Natural quarried stone suits contemporary rigour just as well as the gardens of history. All natural stone is expensive but, if you have a small space, you may consider it worth investing in. Most stone darkens as it weathers, which adds richness and character to the garden. But the immaculate, absorbent limestones or new sandstones will need annual pressure cleaning if you wish to keep their light tone. In deep shade, moss and lichen may be a problem; this too can be resolved chemically but you must avoid run-off into planting beds.

Marble, basalt, granite, sandstone, limestone and slate offer a wide choice of textures and colours – no two flagstones will be the same shade. Choosing the right stone will depend upon the style of the garden as well as the budget. The close-textured, harder or finer stones suit an

far left *Concentric rings of fossilized mussel shells make unusual paving for an area that is hardly walked on. The crystal sphere is lined with gold leaf.*

left *In a modern take on crazy paving, the limestone flooring is distinguished by the textured effect of the jointing pattern made by limestone tesserae.*

Diagonally laid smooth limestone paving surrounds a classically rectangular swimming pool. White pebbles laid in white-tinted concrete provide a non-slip edge that frames the pool.

immaculate garden style best. So if the garden is formally chaste, the stone could be precisely cut granite or glossy Italian marble, its surface smooth and polished. A small courtyard of cool cream limestone or Cumbrian 'green' slate would be minimally elegant. Geometry is served equally well by hard French limestone in shades of yellow, rust and pink, or by granites, with felspar pieces within the stone adding textural appeal. North American quartzite offers rough and close-textured non-slip surfaces, ideal around pools or pathways. In wetter climates all these hard stones would be too slippery, however; the roughened or textured surfaces of riven sandstone would be more appropriate.

The softer, grainy sandstones, for example York stone, are mellow in colour and suit a more relaxed formality. They are usually offered with a natural riven, non-slip finish in seven or eight differently sized rectangular slabs, to be laid in a traditional random jointing pattern. But sandstones are now also available in a smarter, non-riven 'sawn' finish. These look best if units of the same size are used. Rectangular units may be laid in a coursed pattern (explained below and see plan on page 138) and square units in a grid (see photograph on page 21). Both laying patterns are in keeping with the refined plainness of minimalism.

Some natural stones will be found in larger garden centres but for others you will need to contact a specialist stone supplier. Comparative costs may vary according to where you live but some of the larger chains, though having limited choice, do offer reasonable prices.

setts and bricks

Sometimes smaller-unit stone paving suits a space better than large units because it works well around curved edges. Such paving includes cobbles, rounded pebbles and square- or rectangular-cut granite or porphyry setts. The latter, though more expensive, lend themselves best to formally structured gardens. While all can be bought at larger garden centres, a wider choice is available from a stone merchant. Due to their high costs, granite setts are best laid professionally but for small areas you could lay cobbles or pebbles yourself on a concrete base. All create textured patterning at ground level and were usually laid in straight courses, concentric rings or ornamental fan shapes. In modern gardens more elaborate patterns like zigzags or wave patterns are often deployed. A single course of mortared setts could be used to outline large concrete paving slabs, making a lattice pattern across the ground. Small units like bricks may also define grids (see photograph on page 106).

Like stone, clay bricks will always have a role in the garden. While hand-made bricks suit romantic informal gardens best, they would also work in a modern asymmetrical garden outlined by thick timbers or edged by large stones, or used in small groups as 'stepping stones' in a sea of gravel. Otherwise, choose factory-made frostproof brick pavers and lay them in a running bond that ends among plants or runs into fine gravel. This removes the need for ornamental edging, which was the old decorative approach. It is possible to add to the textural effect with lines of contrasting bricks, like hard-fired blue engineering bricks (which can

A shared inner courtyard in a Paris apartment block is paved with coursed red bricks outlined by lengths of white concrete to link seamlessly with the materials of the building. Slim silver birch trunks rise from a platform of clipped Lonicera nitida.

Evenly coloured concrete paving slabs are dry laid without mortar but bark chippings infill the jointing pattern that may eventually host plants.

be more expensive than other colours) with brown, red and mottled ones, or to lay them in lines of varying width.

Bricks can be laid on a base of hardcore and concrete or dry-laid on sand; the latter is less formal in its effect because the bricks are apt to sink slightly. To prevent all small units slipping into a soil bed at either end, it is advisable to build out a 'haunch' of concrete at the end of a row. If planning dwarf box hedging, you will be unable to plant close up to the paving. Frostproof factory bricks cost less than hand-made bricks and are cheaper to buy, but more costly to lay, than stone slabs.

laying and jointing

Traditional paving materials like stone work best when planned with defined straight edges; cutting paving to fit random curves or pointed corners always looks clumsy. Quality stone, usually cut as rectangles, should be laid neatly in parallel with the plan of the garden, even if this is the apparent space. Professional laying is recommended, preferably by a landscaper rather than a builder.

In the modern garden, stone is best laid in a coursed pattern in which length is emphasized and rectangular slabs are laid end to end in parallel. Each course, or line, of paving may be of a different width, with the jointing close-butted across the area – that is, with no gap between slabs – but the courses will be mortared lengthways (see plan on page 138). A formal structure does not mean that everything has to be edged. Unity is now more important, so edges may fade unobtrusively into the garden.

In many cultures grid-based designs have served the garden well and they are even more relevant today. Once seen as a decorative device, the grid is now used as a way of organizing the space. Small units like square clay tiles and brilliantly coloured glazed ceramic tiles are usually laid as a grid (see photograph on page 27); be sure all are frost-hardened if your climate demands it – many terracotta tiles will not withstand frost.

Jointing should reinforce the dynamism of the garden's layout. The linear pattern of coursed jointing emphasizes the order of a formal

split-level courtyard

Terracing solves the problem of a deeply set, enclosed courtyard paved with green slate in which a slate bridge with opaque glass-panelled sides leads to the upper level. Simple planting works all year, the evergreen *Liriope muscari* at basement level being repeated higher up, with parallel rows of velvet-green conifers, *Chamaecyparis obtusa 'Nana'*. Groups of silver birch edge the upper garden and back a bronze sculpture.

In the famous Cubist garden of the Villa Noailles at Hyères, a narrow triangular space is paved with a symmetrical chequerboard of square white concrete frames filled alternately with plants and concrete.

layout. If cut into square units, the flooring becomes more decorative, particularly when laid diagonally, making diamond patterns across the site (see page 21). Mortared jointing may contrast with the colour of the stone but is usually more elegant tinted darker or to match the material. Purpose-made mortar dyes are readily available.

mixing materials

By mixing paving materials the effect at ground level can be considerably enhanced. This is not new: Zen paths used a mixture of unpredictable materials, making the visitor progress carefully, to appreciate the patterns underfoot. What is new is the choice of materials. In the formal context mixing materials should be done either for textural contrast or a contrast of colour, but not both because the effect would jar.

Traditional materials like brick can be given a contemporary look with the addition of narrow bands of slate, and stone or concrete pavers look wonderful with slim strips of steel used as a jointing pattern. In one garden I laid Cumbrian green slate in a coursed pattern and inserted slim strips of highly polished slate between the non-slip, rough-surfaced pavers; these glossy strips dramatically intensified their matt colour. Sometimes flagstones can be softened by filling the jointing with plugs of tender, slow-growing Korean grass (*Zoysia tenuifolia*) or, in cool climates, dwarf thrift (*Armeria caespitosa*), with the bonus of small flowers.

Continuous, 'flowing' materials like concrete, which need expansion joints, may be laid in a large grid pattern by inserting small setts, tiles or bricks, or even narrow lengths of hardwood. Concrete can in fact have anything set into it and there is something very pleasing and restful about such organized schemes. Fired glazed ceramics mix well with stone or marble in a concrete foundation. Square glass bricks (see page 26) inserted into a pattern of matt grey or terracotta tiles have a double function when lights are placed below. And stone, concrete or railway timbers may provide a pattern of stepping stones in gravel.

right *Natural rocks and water
dramatically interrupt smooth strips of
concrete, made to simulate sandstone, in
this garden designed by David Stevens.*

far right *Lilyturf (Ophiopogon)
creates a lattice pattern with square
flagstones set at a diagonal to the
rest of the paving.*

simulated materials

Natural materials are no longer plentiful and their price has risen significantly. In the interest of economy and in order to spare the countryside, manufacturers have developed new materials, such as concrete, that emulate natural ones as well as using reconstituted versions made from chips or powder of the original material. Reconstituted and simulated materials are often also cheaper to lay because they are of a constant thickness, which means that a large area can be laid at a time; provided there is a solid foundation, you should be able to lay these yourself.

The stone flags described on pages 16–17 can all be copied in concrete to make artificial stone but quality remains an all-important consideration. Casts are made to resemble the 'parent' flagstone in every way and the artificial slabs contain crushed stone within the concrete mix, ensuring the right textures and colours. When properly made they will weather as well as the real thing. Be sure to look for the better ones that offer many different sizes so that the duplicated slabs occur less often, and avoid those with a surface full of tell-tale air bubbles and chipped edges around the whole flagstone, which are entirely unconvincing. Good manufacturers will choose old stones of character for the casts, perhaps even with chisel markings relating to how the original stones were quarried or used. Any colour should run evenly through the thickness of the stone so that wearing away will not change the look.

Concrete can also be used to simulate terracotta pavers for areas where frost is a problem. These may take time to mellow, and where the pavers are all exactly the same shade the result is very artificial. Some suppliers have produced pleasing effects by casting from real terracotta tiles but aiming to create the individual look produced by firing, in which there will be scrape marks and a few punctured bubble holes. Some will be rough, some smooth and in shape they will look hand-made, which adds piquancy to strict formality. Sometimes a group of tiles is cast into a larger unit, reducing the cost; careful jointing can make them look effective and time will soften the newness to an extent. All can be laid in the modern pattern of coursed lines running in parallel, rather than the fussier chevron or basketweave patterns of the past.

Concrete 'bricks' are also available and all the reservations and virtues referred to above will apply. Some look almost genuine, with dragged surfaces and broody colouring, but you will need to beware of some horribly inauthentic colours. Clay bricks are rust-red, not the purple-red so often used in simulated brick or concrete pavers. Grey concrete 'setts' work well, particularly those with a pumice-stone surface, and there are some textured, cream-coloured setts that resemble the surface of travertine marble. They can be allowed to weather or may be pressure-cleaned once a year to maintain their pristine, pale appearance.

Some coarse concrete setts are of different sizes and are tumbled to break the manufactured perfection. They weather well and can be laid in geometric patterns if the area is large, such as a drive. To my mind there is nothing wrong with honest concrete slabs of an even grey or cream; they may have a stratified surface to make them safer and can look pleasantly regular for the modern formal garden.

materials that flow

Modern technology has changed the face of flooring. Some paving materials come directly as spin-offs from the chemical industries, others are salvaged. As we shall see, more contemporary gardens look inwards than outwards and the materials chosen may lead the design rather than follow. There are some wonderful new materials that will flow and set to fill any curve or awkward corner; wet-poured on site, they harden to make a durable surface. Loose-laid gravel too is still popular as a flooring material to flow around the site (see pages 4 and 146).

gravel

By no means a new material for the garden, gravel has in the past been used in an entirely decorative way. Parterres and knot gardens were often filled with coloured gravels in place of plants as part of the ornamental style. Today gravel has a more practical use as flooring, albeit one difficult to walk on. It can also act as a moisture-retaining mulch in a planting bed or as a weed suppressant. And plants that revel in full sunshine and freely draining soil often need a cool root run. These requirements make gravel a versatile and attractive material for the contemporary gardener.

From a design point of view, the strict order of Japanese gardens, in which gravel is a common material, has led to its use in a modern formal context. The flowing seas of gravel that swirl around minimal planting in oriental gardens have struck a note in the West. Sometimes even the meticulous daily raking, as in the Japanese context, has influenced the contemporary designer (see photograph on page 147). Flows of gravel will easily cover any part of the site, however small or awkward the shape, and it is not expensive to buy or to lay. So aggregates are well suited to the ideals of the minimalist garden or modern formality in which the texture fills whole areas without over-complicating a design.

There are several types of gravel, varying also in size from small (6mm/less than ⅛in) through to large (20mm/¾in). Sharp-edged chippings come from crushed rock and rounded pea shingle usually from a beach or river; the former tend to move less than the latter. All gravels must be washed before they are used in the garden. The colours are natural and vary from pale tones that suit minimalist elegance (though I would avoid pure white quartz with its funereal connotations) to darker hues. There are warm reds, pinks, blue-greys and greens, all of which are gentle associates with plants. Try to choose colours that do not contrast with the rest of the hard landscape or buildings. Textural contrast, however, is important. The softest effect is achieved by using a mix of brown with cream or honey colours. Ask for samples from the nursery or stone supplier to see which size or colour you prefer.

As a mulch over spare planting, gravel is best laid over a sheet of permeable horticultural textile to prevent weeds from seeding through. Cut small crossed slits in the textile, plant through these, then cover the whole surface with a layer of gravel, 50mm (2in) thick or slightly more.

concrete

Of all contemporary materials, concrete is one that will follow any course without interruption. In terms of building, it was *the* material of the twentieth century, but in the garden we have been slow to take advantage of its properties. Concrete is hard-wearing, economical and in small areas simple to lay, though there must always be an edge restraint and jointing to allow for expansion. Provided the ground is level, this fluid material will fill any shape and it may be painted with flooring paint, stained with dye or textured, making it the most versatile contemporary surface of all.

above left *Shapes of randomly cut white marble are set into large squares of black polished concrete paving and bench seats, making a light-hearted confetti effect in this 'gardens of shadows' in a Paris park. Round the trees, square stainless steel grilles are slit randomly to allow water through and mix well with the scheme.*

above right *In an unusual garden designed by Andrew Cao, the ground is as undulating as in the natural landscape. Resin-bonded glass chippings, graded in colour from yellow 'hills' through green 'slopes' to a deep blue 'valley', follow its form. The enclosing walls are coated with blue glass chippings.*

If colour is added when concrete is freshly worked, it will run evenly through the material, so the tint is constant and chipping not a problem. Equally, concrete can be stained by tints that have a chemical reaction to give it a permanent immaculate, silken finish that suits crisp, modern garden styles. Smooth concrete may also be polished to make a glossy patina with a light-reflective surface. Colouring the concrete, as well as laying it in large areas, must be done by a professional. Colours may be vibrantly suited to brilliant sunlit areas and a foil for exotic planting such as yuccas and hardy fan palms, or they can be gentle earth tones from beige to dusty terracotta pink to charcoal blue-grey; these set off green foliage and luminous pastel flowers. In all cases the technology has developed to cope with a freeze–thaw situation.

Alternatively, the surface of concrete may be rippled or grooved as the concrete sets ('goes off') by imprinting it with a length of timber before it hardens. The friction caused by such textures has a practical advantage and can also affect the colour intensity. The surface may be further textured using natural aggregates, like crushed stone gravels, to give a rough effect; add them to the concrete while it is being mixed. Depending on their size, gravels can create smoother or grittier effects; select their colours (see page 22) to suit the buildings or to work with the planting style. As the concrete sets, use a stiff brush to remove the smooth surface and to expose the gritty texture of the aggregate.

resin bonding

A more recent material that will also flow to fill any shape involves laying gravels in epoxy resin. In this case, the texture of the aggregate is much denser than with concrete and the visual effect is closer to that of loose-laid gravel. Though it is more expensive than using aggregate in concrete, resin bonding answers some of the problems encountered with loose gravels: for example, falling leaves in autumn may be brushed or hosed from the surface of bonded gravel, and the surface is silent compared with the crunch of loose stones – though this may be a drawback for those who like to hear the approach of people or cars.

Bonded gravels are more functional and more durable than loose-laid material and will follow every detailed curve or narrowed form that a designer has planned. Sometimes the bonded material is edged with setts or stone or a retaining slim timber while setting. Once 'cured', no visible edging is necessary, though evergreens like low spreading cotoneasters, creeping junipers and *Lonicera pileata* can be used to soften the edges.

A resin-bonded surface is easily and quickly laid, but professional laying is essential, using the best quality mix. The underlying foundations for bonded surfaces may be concrete, asphalt or timber; they must be well compacted and absolutely clean, with no loose material, to ensure perfect curing (see photograph on page 114). For heavy vehicle use, like a drive, the laying technique is slightly different, to provide a more

24

far left *Detail of a design by Bonita Bulaitis shows an immaculate stretch of bonded cream gravel that flows easily around planted areas and inset crosses of stainless steel, while maintaining a sharp edge.*

left *Luminous pale blue glass chippings make a spiral ridge in a clear pool. The line emerges from a sculpted head to swirl into a vortex within a ring of the ornamental grass, Carex 'Frosted Curls'.*

Wide lengths of concrete are imaginatively used to provide an enticing garden entrance, over a still lily pool and between concrete walls. Diagonal slits replace expansion joints, giving the illusion that the slabs float on water.

industrial inspiration

Scaffolding sets a three-dimensional framework for a garden in which glass bricks, merging with pale concrete pavers, are used both as flooring and boundary. Blond limestone gravel gives variety and provides a well-drained bed for sparely planted fescues. The sense of enclosure is completed by the stretched blue canvas, making a backcloth for the erect, orange and cream *Kniphofia* 'Shining Sceptre' in shiny metal containers. Other evergreen plants, a bamboo (*Fargesia murieliae*) and the climber *Trachelospermum jasminoides* soften the stark materials.

right *A metal grid provides a secure, yet transparent bridge across a pool.*

far right *Enclosing a courtyard designed by Juan Grimm, this massive, coarsely rendered wall allows junipers to run through its low 'window'. The bold grid of the floor defines perfect squares infilled with diagonally placed granite setts, while the terracotta tiles bordering them match the colour of the roof and palely echo that of the wall.*

durable and flexible surface. The result is an immaculate surface that blends with modern building materials and with all types of planting.

Not all aggregates are natural. All sorts of loose materials, new to garden use, can be resin-bonded. Resins look exciting when used with glass chippings, whose colours range from rich hues like deep blue to the more luminous pale tones. Crushed glass is not dangerously sharp due to its processing by the recycling industries. But for really brilliant colour, nothing can beat a surface made from recycled chopped rubber, used as a filler and resin-bonded, and there are some dramatic modern gardens using this durable surface. Initially developed for sports surfaces, being soft and resilient, it is ideal for areas where children or bare feet may walk, such as around swimming pools. It flows with the same precision as the materials described above and, since it adheres well, will cover steep mounds or overhangs; it must be professionally laid. It stands heavy wear and is free-draining, while the colour opens up imaginative treatments.

Plastic chippings, coloured sands, round coloured glass beads, broken ceramics and coloured pebbles provide exciting fillers for resin-bonded surfaces; they may also be set into concrete. If the result is ornamental, use them only for small areas, rather like the shell grottoes of the past, since too much patterning can be difficult to set into modern formality.

Some materials normally associated with industrial sites have come into the garden recently. They particularly suit a minimal or 'high tech' garden style and complement modern architecture. You may need to approach a building contractor to obtain some of these materials or they can be bought direct from architectural suppliers or large builder's merchants.

Aluminium footplates with a friction surface pattern are used for metal decks, which need professional installation. They suit dramatic achromatic designs with white walls, black-painted timbers, glass and steel. The style of planting should be in character. Dark foliage such as that of *Ophiopogon planiscapus* 'Nigrescens', a 30cm (12in) high grassy plant, picks up the gauntlet, while the taller *Artemisia canescens* is wire-like and the huge biennial *Onopordum acanthium* could have been cut from a sheet of steel. All this is boldly uncompromising in its effect.

The type of metal mesh found in the engine room of large ships has been used successfully in modern gardens for walkways, staircases and balconies; it is both sturdy and weatherproof. Transparent mesh bridges over water or plants will allow people to look through as they traverse. All these metal surfaces and finishes mix well with white or pale grey gravels or contrast effectively with cool grey timber decking.

*Provided there is a comfortable walking surface, a
path need not be flat. It can swing out into space with
three-dimensional dynamism, like this red timber path
by Charles Jencks.*

soft & sensual

The feet are sorely tested in metropolitan life. Even the most extreme
modern garden with uncompromising formal lines should be welcoming.
There is, therefore, always a place for grass or other soft, tactile floorings
such as wooden decks.

grass

Fluid curves or awkward shapes that come to a point can be excellently
filled by grass or chopped bark. In town gardens grass is often rejected
because of the problem of storing a mower but bark is a magnet for
birds so, while it may start formal, it will end up looking very messy.
Either may be replaced by gravel (see page 22), that will flow over
walking surfaces and continue uninterrupted around plants as a mulch,
but you cannot lie down on gravel and it lacks the fresh fragrance of
newly cut grass.

Grass, however, stays manageable and a compact carpet of
immaculately mown turf will fit in with a small formal garden as a rug
will soften a wooden floor. More adventurously, grass may be sown to
fill alternate squares of a ground-level grid pattern, with bright green
areas alternating with the grey of gravel (rather as helxine is used in the
photograph on page 90); this should preferably be done in an area that
is little walked on, or the grass and gravel may intermingle. Even in a tiny
formal space, grass can be used to make linear patterns that texture the
floor (see page 116). For such perfection, choose the finest quality grass
seed and be prepared to mow once a week in the growing season.

If you have large areas of grass, enormous fun can be had by
adjusting the height of the blades and using the mower to define
geometric patterns, rectangles, key patterns, curvaceous wave patterns,
concentric circles or even ground mazes. You will need to mark out the

opposite *Mown grass provides the tactile medium for a
contemporary turf maze based on concentric circles.
Enclosed within a circular hedge and with a central
specimen tree, it still evokes a spiritual atmosphere.*

patterns on the ground using pegs and string for circles or straight lines.
Once made, the lines will be simple to follow or the pattern may be
changed at will.

decking

Decking is a pleasant alternative to hard stone and a smooth deck is kind
to bare feet. Though not new, decking is becoming more popular even in
those countries which have a wet climate, and as a linear material it is
well suited to formality. In association with concrete, stone or tiles,

decking will relate well to modern buildings and it looks superb when cantilevered out over water. The timber should be either hardwood or pressure-treated softwood; it may be coloured by paint or given subtle staining effects. Hardwoods should be from renewable sources. Look for Scandinavian redwood, which is the most economical and stays a brownish colour. Western red cedar is a traditional, medium-priced decking material, while the most expensive, American white oak, is denser and therefore heavier. The latter two weather to an attractive, soft silver-grey colour.

One of the best characteristics of timber decks is that the whole extended outdoor living area of the house can be built from the same material. Benches and rails may line the perimeter, with overhead shade-giving pergolas constructed of the same timber; tables too may be built in. Steps from the house or into the rest of the garden will be made from the same wood, giving a pleasing homogeneity. The only contrast may lie in the pattern made by laying the planks at different angles, or by choosing planks of different widths. Where there is a level change or steps, however, the wood could be laid in a different direction. A house is set off well if the timber is laid at right angles to its walls, unless there are steps down on to the deck, in which case long horizontals would suit better. Introducing diagonals makes for slightly less order but adds to the creative tension. Decking is usually planned very geometrically and the repeat pattern is part of its charm. The defined edges need not be abrupt but may fade discreetly into the rest of the garden.

Where timber decking joins the main building it is advisable to consider a drainage channel. Decks are raised above ground over either a concreted floor or an area covered with black plastic sheet concealed beneath a good layer of gravel, so that weeds will not come through. The upright posts, on which the joists and beams are laid, must be set in concrete footings and all nails or brackets should be galvanized. For damp climates, be aware that wet timber decks are slippery: precision-grooved timber planks are available or a coloured resin/aggregate overlay may be bonded to the wooden surface, ensuring a better grip. Inexpensive modular decking units can now be bought as large 'tiles', but I prefer to see decking displayed in long lines, either at right angles or set diagonally, than to have the pattern further broken into square units.

far left **Decking is usually planned very geometrically and here it creates linear patterns with random edges that get 'lost' in the planting. The apparent width of this deck is doubled by its immaculate reflection in the sliding glass doors.**

left **Beautiful detailing enhances this natural timber paving, the wide slats being edged with wooden pegs and infilled with gravel.**

architecturally led

In this simple roof garden designed by architect Ian Chee, wooden decking is used to soften the galvanized steel construction. Less formal stepping stones of concrete and natural boulders also contrast with the minimalist building and bring a sense of mountainous elevation to the garden, echoed by the contained mountain pines (*Pinus mugo Pumilio Group*).

boundaries

Most boundaries are intended for complete seclusion, but others may be chosen to reveal a view or to let in light. Divisions of internal space can be just as important as those which define the territory of the garden. All vertical structures in the formal garden should be compatible with the selected floor material, without too much contrast in texture and colour.

walls

Traditional methods of building walls using stone or bricks are relevant to modern gardens but variations can be included to give a more contemporary feel, provided they simplify the overall effect and avoid the rustic. Before building any solid walling, seek the advice of a professional.

brick

Blue-black engineering bricks make dark walls that accommodate well to concrete and glass architecture. Gaps can be planned to frame a view, if you have one, rather as Japanese 'moon gates' pierced solid walls. Mortar may be coloured, either lighter or darker, to contrast with the brickwork and emphasize the pattern. Never paint brick unless it is really unattractive as you will not be able to remove the paint in the future without destroying the brick surface. If the brickwork has already been spoiled by peeled and stained paint, or if it is in poor condition, consider rendering with a sand-cement (concrete) mix.

rendering

Rendering is an invaluable way to camouflage either messy brickwork or inexpensive pre-cast concrete blocks if these have been used to enclose or divide garden space. It involves covering a surface with a thin layer of concrete to give an all-over plain background and has the advantage of concealing all jointing, offering an opportunity for a continuous, smooth wall. A rendered surface may be smoothly finished, almost to a glassy perfection, or left fairly coarse. The mix must be frost-resistant, so allow it to set slowly in damp, rather than hot, dry conditions. It can be left uncoloured, or either painted or stained. Imitating stucco brings back the classical world, so strong earth reds, terracotta and ochre yellows are appropriate colours.

There are many wall shrubs that would be well suited to such a simple backcloth and training them to lie flat gives a spare, contemporary feel. The flowering ornamental quince (*Chaenomeles*), for example, has a naturally elegant habit and can also be trained to lie flat against the wall where, even in winter, it looks stylish because of the black pattern made by the branches. In warmer climates the floriferous Mexican shrub *Cestrum elegans* also has a graceful stemmed habit. Depending on the wall colour, consider choosing a white chaenomeles for a strongly coloured background or wine-coloured *Cestrum roseum* 'Ilnacullin' on a luminously pale one. Against a strongly coloured stucco wall a more robust character such as a fan-trained fig, *Ficus carica* 'Brown Turkey', would hold its own. Bear in mind that any wall shrubs will conceal part of the wall and make repainting difficult. For the minimalist garden, the plain wall may well be enough. Rendering and painting a wall can be carried out by a practical amateur with some experience of DIY.

stone

All stone is expensive, but precision-finished, finely mortared limestone looks wonderful in the modern context. Cladding concrete blocks with sheets of marble or slate is a cheaper way of achieving the same effect at a fraction of the cost (see photograph on page 41). The softer stones, like

above left *A pink-washed 'distressed' undulating concrete surface makes a dominating wall with a flood of small pebbles at floor level.*

above right *Glassily clear water reveals the natural stone wall behind, made of slim slivers of flat sandstone laid horizontally.*

limestone or sandstone, are easy to work with and can be dressed to a sophisticated finish, which suits the modern formal garden. You will find some stones in garden centres, but for real choice go to a stone supplier, who will advise on suitability.

Dry stone walling, that is without mortar, does not generally suit the formal ethic. Mortared jointing can be carried out so that the jointing is not emphasized, or you can make much of the coursing pattern by using raked joints, which adds shadow and makes a wall look substantial. Dry stone techniques, however, may have a place in the simple minimal garden where the texture will be appreciated – and a wall of river pebbles is quite beautiful when well made. Be sure a stone wall stands on a good foundation of concrete; building a high boundary takes professional skill.

A detail from a garden designed by Dan Kiley shows a pristine wall of horizontal concrete panels fringed by wisteria, whose twining stems grow up taut wires. In the central island, a mat of dwarf lilyturf (Ophiopogon japonicus 'Minor') surrounds clipped azaleas.

fences

The word fencing tends to conjure up a rural image, such as white-painted pickets or ranch-like post-and-rail, neither of which is appropriate to the modern theme. But there are other ways of using timber to create a sharper, more geometric concept. The simplest system usually provides the best formal frame and can be carried out quite easily, provided good materials are used and the posts are set into a concrete base. This is not costly, but avoid the cheapest wood and be sure that the timber you use is guaranteed pressure-treated against weathering.

In the modern context, fencing may be made from materials other than wood and metals are perhaps the most appropriate. Panels can be made of sheet metal, with perforated designs, or from steel mesh. Alternatively, steel rods, aluminium slats or copper pipes may be used vertically, horizontally or even diagonally. Cast or wrought iron still has a role too, though not in the traditionally ornate manner.

timber

It is well worth having fence panels specially made for you by a carpenter, in which case the initial decision is whether to choose hardwoods or pressure-treated softwoods. The former – like cedar, redwood and oak – looks after itself, ageing to a soft, pale grey. The latter opens up different design opportunities such as using painted colour or grain-revealing stains. Pressure-treated softwood timbers will last for many years and they make immaculate stylish fencing when sealed or painted. There is no limit to the different patterns possible based upon the vertical timber theme. Square- or rectangular-section laths or rounded poles may be used: these may be thick or thin, spaced or butted, erect, horizontal or diagonal, painted or stained. Wide laths can be interspersed with others of different thickness, or they may be laid horizontally, with slim spacings. Very slim laths with a square section make a pleasingly light screen when closely and evenly spaced.

right *At the Chaumont Garden Festival in France's Loire
Valley, an original garden is enclosed by woven willow
walls that creak and bend like the sides of a huge basket.*

centre right *A beautiful timber trellis is made from
square-section laths, paired vertically and horizontally.*

far right *The screen of slim silver-birch branches has a
natural irregularity which softens the enclosure's formality
and links with the birch trees beyond.*

Where the strong effects of rough materials like concrete or granite setts have been chosen for paving, the coarseness of railway sleepers becomes a virtue. The solid textured surface is weatherproof and durable, requiring no treatment. Laid horizontally, such timbers can be used to retain banked earth, which is an economical way of making raised planters or terracing difficult levels. Fixing with galvanized screws and building with a very slight batter ensures a long-lasting retaining wall. Both hardwoods and softwoods can be planed smooth for a more refined look.

Mixing other materials with timber is striking in a garden where detail may otherwise be sparse. The character of the garden will indicate which materials mix best and you would need to consult a landscape contractor to have such fencing made up. Planed hardwood timber laths spaced alternately with shiny steel strips can set up rhythmical vertical patterns around a tailored garden space. For a finer look, panels of split bamboo in a frame of painted timber add an oriental influence.

metal

Metal is a chic but practical material for contemporary gardens; because it is strong it can be delicately wrought or cast. Galvanized metal – aluminium or steel – has superseded the black iron railings of the past.

Its inventive use produces bent and twisted pre-formed railings that make patterns; these can be purchased ready-made from fencing companies. Just one twist in a straight rod, copied in each railing at a progressively higher level, makes a plain railed fence take on a rhythmical character. Or a flowing pattern may be made by panels that lean alternately forward and backward, altering its appearance as you pass by. Traditional finials have no place in the contemporary garden but metal craftsmen will design bespoke metal fences with hand-crafted bronze or brass detailing.

Metals may be painted with brilliant colour or with paler, faded tones to give a more subtle appearance. They can be coated with metal powders, different from the main material and adding richness to it. Alternatively, rails and rods may be sealed, galvanized or left to verdigris, depending on the metal.

Trellis can also be wrought from metals like stainless steel or copper, making a starkly minimalist statement. Polished stainless steel may be used to build an open, large-scale trellis, which, sited against a rendered coloured wall, is enough in itself, sculpturally independent of climbing plants. Pierced steel grilles or finely woven wire mesh panels in different gauges also have no need of plants but they provide sturdy, burglarproof screens while allowing light through. Galvanized corrugated metal

rhythms of light

Designed by Topher Delaney with elegantly judged simplicity, the fence is made from flat sections of blue-painted steel, without cross bars but closely spaced for safety. This contemporary material clearly defines the boundary without obscuring the view and creates strong rhythmical shadow patterns on the smooth drive. Seen through the fence, the wonderful prospect over woodland becomes part of the garden.

sheeting will add style to very modern gardens but, though immaculate when new, it becomes rustic and 'distressed' when weathered. Flattened copper tubing will verdigris but this is its attractive quality. When woven and twisted, sited against brick or a painted background, this is another material best displayed without plants. Any specially commissioned metal work will be costly, but some creative work is available more cheaply as ready-made panels from metal fencing companies.

The most invisible of metal fencing is tensioned yachting wire, stretched between metal posts. Rather like using thin wire to support the illusion of moving puppets, steel wire is barely seen in the garden, yet it provides worthy plant support. The high tensile strength is sufficient to carry even heavy climbers like *Wisteria sinensis* or *Clematis montana*. Safety on roof gardens is another use for tensioned wire because it will not break – but it allows wind through which can have a devastating effect on plants. Thick rope is another alternative but, however it is stretched, it will never have the crispness of tensioned wire.

translucent boundaries

Complete transparency may be desirable beside the sea or looking on to open countryside but, as always in gardens, wind protection is vital. On roof gardens or in urban spaces silicone-bonded glass, ordered from a glass supply company, is expensive but wonderfully effective, particularly when part of it is acid-etched and opaque. A similar but lighter-weight effect can be achieved using cheaper polycarbonate sheeting, available from builder's merchants, that resists ultraviolet degradation. Frosted perspex creates complete seclusion too. Plants grown beside these will get enough light but they should be well shaped to make the most of the silhouette effect. Horizontally tiered *Cornus controversa* 'Variegata', duplicated mounds of rounded whipcord hebes or one sculpted cloud topiary of *Ilex crenata* are good candidates, as are massed herbaceous plants like the narrowly erect *Digitalis ferruginea* or *Eremurus bungei*.

For more solid effects make translucent walls of glass bricks (see photograph on page 26), which can readily be bought from architectural suppliers. There are many different patterns and the light through these has a sharper quality. Glass bricks are very strong and may be mortared together like ordinary bricks. They would fit very well with concrete, coloured or not, and stone.

top *Woven and riveted flattened copper tubing, ingeniously designed by Julia Brett, makes a striking trellis, with* Acer palmatum 'Sango-kaku' *showing through.*

above *Panels of stainless steel mesh make an elegant and secure fence, designed by Eva Jiricna.*

features

Besides giving a wonderful opportunity to get close to
nature, gardens are also places of rest and movement.
Their design may invite us to explore but every garden should
include somewhere to pause and reflect. In the geometrically
planned garden there will be areas where routes open out,
paths converge or a simple focal point becomes necessary
to turn our attention inwards. And in the asymmetric, more
abstractly shaped garden there is also a desire to provide
an area of stillness. When at peace, contemplating pleasing
detail is an intrinsic part of the garden experience. So the
choice of furnishing, shelter for relaxing, the inclusion and
style of water, the way the garden is lit at night and the
focal-point details like containers and sculpture make an
important contribution. All such features need to be
integrated as a logical and pleasing extension of the
garden's formal character.

The simple circular pavilion is a place to pause amidst the textures of a wild
meadow and with a view over the surrounding lush countryside.

Pristine white moulded plastic furniture provides a place to eat on an elegantly simple terrace designed by Richard Unsworth. It associates well with large concrete containers for phormiums and a small pool for pygmy water lilies.

furniture

What people want from the modern formal garden is no different from the requirements of all gardens, past and present – namely, comfort, practicability and beauty. The style of furniture should be in keeping with the spirit of the garden, so for spaces planned on geometric principles, simple shapes and lines are essential; elaborate ornamental designs have no role here. There are new materials to choose from as well as different ways of using traditional materials that suit the elegance of contemporary modernity. Bespoke furniture, crafted by a designer, can often double as sculpture but if you intend to sit in it, make sure that comfort is not sacrificed to style. While creativity and inventiveness take us forward, sheer opportunism has taught us to make use of salvage, so we now see seats made from marble slabs, old stone lintels or sections of stone pillar.

If furniture is sited as an important focus of the design, it must be solidly visible when viewed from a distance, both structurally and in terms of its colour. Such seats may have a massive grandeur or a strikingly dominant form and pale tones will stand out best from afar. In more intimate or enclosed spaces, seats may be tucked out of sight and 'happened upon', in which case they can be designed with a lighter touch. Seating that is planned to be more low-key might be made from lightweight aluminium, slatted metal or wirework so that it is semi-transparent. If built in, a simple bench could be supported by two low walls of glass bricks.

concrete

In a formally planned space, furniture is often best as an integral, fitted part of the design, permanently fixed in its space: concrete is an ideal material here. In truly minimalist style, the concrete used would be identical to that of the paving and built in as part of the garden's

right *Hinge-mounted against a smooth concrete wall, a plain wooden bench is a space-saving way to offer rest.*

far right *The built-in seat of pale limestone cladding against a blockwork wall makes a pleasant corner to sit in the sun without disrupting the garden's formal unity.*

architectural structure. Cast concrete can be used with finely ground stone filler, making it simulate the look of real stone, or the surface can be coloured or textured, as it is for paving (see page 24).

Garden seating need no longer be constructed upon the principle of a bench, with a rectangular base supported by four legs: in the twenty-first century the inspiration is just as likely to come from the streamlined structure of aerodynamics. Formed as a pourable liquid, concrete can be moulded around a steel armature to make all manner of fluid or geometric shapes. Benches cantilevered from the wall are space-saving and may incorporate smooth 'tables' at either end. Or a thick ribbon of concrete can be moulded to make a sinuous serpentine curve, touching the ground in only two places. All concrete must be well mixed and slowly cured while damp, but most of these ideas will be made on site by a craftsman as a commission. This versatile material will weather like stone and darken slightly with age, but it can be pressure-cleaned if you wish to preserve its pristine look.

metal

For the geometric garden that is uncompromisingly modern, substantial metal furniture, anchored in place, has a role to play. The difference between modern steel and the cast iron of the past is the ratio of improved strength to a slimmer framework. There are sturdy possibilities for architect-designed cantilevered or slim, linear shapes, using chromed or lacquered steel. But a wide variety of freestanding metal furniture can

be purchased ready-made and is very affordable compared with designer-made originals. Modern tables and chairs made of corrosive-resistant stainless steel may have a satinized or glassily chromed finish or be perforated to give a lacy effect. Galvanized metals like iron or mild steel do not rust outdoors, which makes them suitable for garden use; all fixings should be brass or chromed.

The new metal alloys may be powder-coated with colour, extending the range of hues to include silver, green, blue and red, and providing a longer-lasting surface than by simply painting them. And metal can be made to look lighter than it is, if made from high-strength aluminium alloy with seats and backs of galvanized wire mesh. Or a contrast can be provided when the metal is combined with timber slats, woven plastics or coloured glass-fibre resins. For comfort, plain woven or calico cushions are an essential addition to all-metal furniture.

timber

Freestanding timber furniture will always be around; it lends itself well to the simple lines of contemporary formality and is convenient for alfresco eating. Movable pieces allow you to change completely the dynamics of the garden space.

Timber seating should preferably be made from sustainable hardwoods but pressure-treated softwoods are an alternative if they are to be painted. Be aware that there is tannin in hardwoods and this may exude for up to a year, during which time it could stain pale flooring.

Where the garden is small, wooden seating may be built in as part of the framework of the site. In place of the old, heavy cast iron frames, bench seating is often mounted on aluminium or black tubular legs or light steel arches, or a seat may be cantilevered from a firmly set metal or concrete base. If the bench is all wood, it must stand on stone or concrete flooring, as even treated timber lasts better when not in contact with damp ground.

Hardwood seats and tables may be left outdoors through the year but it is better to bring painted furniture inside for the winter. Hot sunlight, as well as wet and frost, affects all timber, so maintenance should be carried out once a year, treating the wood with preservative or repainting it. If the furniture is made of cedar or oak this should not be necessary, as both weather to a desirable pale grey. Check any metal fixings for rust.

There are many craftsmen working in wood now offering distinctive and original furniture and their work may be seen at the large garden shows; many advertise in garden magazines. This furniture is not mass-produced so it will be costly. Breaking with tradition has produced attractive new ranges of ready-made wooden furniture too. Using pressure and steam treatment, timber bench seats are available with an undulating surface, allowing each person to sit on a smooth dip. There are also elegant seats with classical allusions, symmetrical and with scrolled ends. You could even commission a carpenter to make a curved meandering bench from planed timber to wind around your site.

below left **This chic minimalist urban garden, designed by Stephen Woodhams, benefits from transparent inflatable furniture that is easily dismantled.**

below centre **Slatted timber deckchairs suit formal courtyards just as well as boat decks, the shadows making a linear design on brick paving. The addition of cushions would improve comfort.**

below right **The bench has been reinvented for the contemporary garden. Here an undulating slatted-wood seat on a lightweight steel frame looks immaculate in front of a grey stone-clad wall in a pristine garden space.**

Surrounded by woodland, a two-tier timber deck ingeniously provides a fitted table surrounded by seating, over which the tree furnishes dappled shade. Minimalist planting of irises and Stipa tenuifolia grow from rounded river pebbles.

Living wood furniture has also attained a new popularity. The old craft of willow weaving has been revived but the shapes are bolder than the 'basket' traditions of the past. Within the modernity of contemporary formal gardens the contorted irregularities provide a dramatic contrast with immaculately managed hard materials. As privacy is often important in the urban garden, an arbour – that is, a covered seat cocooned within a ceiling and walls – will offer both shade and seclusion. Canes and willow can be wrought into the most satisfying shapes, with extended arms and a roof. A modern arbour made from woven willow may be even bought in kit form, comprising a seat within a curved roof.

plastics

Durable plastic is available for everyone, but the price will reflect the quality. At the inexpensive end of the market plastics are often cast as reproduction shapes, imitating those that were once cast iron. These tend to be vulnerable to frost and ultraviolet light in summer, which makes them crack. And if your garden is exposed, lightweight furniture will dance away with the wind.

High-quality plastic furniture is more durable, though more expensive. Designs that respect the liquid nature of the cast material can be elegant and modern, with great purity of line. These plastics can be pre-formed, strengthened with glass fibre and moulded into an organically flowing shape. The base of a chair, for example, may be a rounded 'pool' from which a single stem, with great tensile strength, supports the curved seat and back. Today there is a revival of the boldness of 1950s and 1960s designs, using the new plastics. There are matt surfaces in sophisticated white, black and grey for the garden of restrained formality; bright colour will suit the ethic of the modern garden in which restraint is not a theme.

garden buildings & structures

Many gardens fulfil the need for a retreat. This could take the form of a small extension, leaning on the house wall, or a freestanding summer house, pavilion, gazebo or even purpose-built studio. If not hidden away, such a building is best planned as a part of the garden style, in proportion with the space and scaled for people. In gardens of a formal design, nostalgic or rustic styles are out, but there are many contemporary designs using traditional or new materials.

pergolas and arches

Overhead shade and plant supports were always a part of the traditional garden. Timber was the usual material for pergola walkways, supported by either heavy brick piers or wooden posts. The same pleasures are sought today but metal is now the material most often used. The overall look of a pergola has otherwise changed little, however, being either simply rectangular or arched, although the scale and proportion will be somewhat reduced in the modern versions. Today's pergolas also tend to be less elaborate than previously, with fewer plants.

Some arches and pergolas are simple to install and economic, being made of lightweight aluminium, coated with plastic. These simple arched frames can be pushed into the soil and, provided lightweight plants are grown over them, they will withstand wind. The original single, wide iron hoops of the past enabled expansive arabesques of twining climbers to soar overhead; these suit contemporary formal styling just as well and may cross wide paths. Clematis are the ideal climbers for this situation: avoid planting in a frost pocket and ensure that the roots are shaded.

If you intend a pergola to carry heavier climbers, the posts must be strong enough and tall enough, preferably 2.5m (8ft), to allow weighty climbers like wisteria or roses to trail clear of the head of a person below.

If made of timber, the beams and rafters should be deep (150–200mm/ 6–8in) with an average thickness of 50mm (2in), to avoid warping. Bases should be firmly secured in concrete in the ground, against high winds.

For a modern house made of concrete, glass and steel, the architectural value of using heavier 'construction' steel beams (usually hidden inside concrete) for a pergola is that the garden will relate clearly to it. These structural beams tie house and garden together, defining line and indicating three-dimensional volume with great simplicity. Scaffolding will achieve the same purpose more economically, with a lighter intention.

A pergola is usually open on both sides but in some contemporary gardens it may be on the perimeter, so one side may be panelled to conceal an unattractive view. Along the boundary, mistily opaque etched glass or polycarbonate panels will allow light through or stainless steel mesh create ground-level shadow patterns along the length of the walk. Taut canvas may also be used stretched overhead for screening. In the absence of overhead cover, however, consider the dramatic foliage of large-leaved climbers like golden hop (*Humulus lupulus* 'Aureus') or the massive-leaved Japanese glory vine (*Vitis coignetiae*).

canopies and awnings

No garden should be uncomfortable and all that may be needed where people sit is a means of filtering the light. In hot areas canopies protect people from the sun while allowing some light through. Translucent or opaque fabric panels can be made from canvas, flame-resistant PVC-coated polyester, coated glass cloth or other materials that can withstand wind and weather and are not too costly. Flimsy, muslin-like fabric may be draped like blinds, strung over taut yachting wire or rolled back over a timber dowel to protect a seating area from the midday sun.

*A blue-painted blue wooden pergola and trellis define a geometric arbour
raised above the lawn and reached via railway-sleeper steps.*

*Isabelle Greene designed this substantial timber pergola set against
gleaming white-rendered walls. Rafters made from thick poles sit on heavy
rounded beams as bulky as a mast on a sailing boat.*

A wooden deck designed by architect Gabriele Poole, with its timbers running parallel to the glass walls and doors of a contemporary house, is screened overhead with taut canvas awnings. The diagonal thrust of the metal supports has an almost cantilevered effect; they are matched by the metal mesh seating running along the perimeter of the terrace. Plain furnishings in black and cream maintain a formal simplicity. Permanent canopies like this require considered fabric engineering, using tension wires and ropes, which is an expensive undertaking; there are manufacturers who specialize in this. The materials are welded or stitched together, and the awning supported on a strong frame of reinforced steel.

modern verandah

summer houses

If a summer house is visible, the construction will dominate the view unless it is made from the same material as the house. Or it may be pale, if made from painted timber, or transparent if largely glass, both of which can be a foil for a more dramatic-looking feature or architectural plant in front. Freestanding summer houses are usually rectangular, hexagonal, square, octagonal or circular in shape; the basic geometry is best kept simple, with little adornment. You could have a custom-made summer house designed by an architect or craftsman, as a feature to suit the mood of the garden. Views out need to be considered when siting a summer house – you want to look at an attractive scene from your retreat. Another possibility is to put it on a turntable, to follow the warmth of the sun. The back can be used for the storage of garden implements and will do away with the need for a shed.

In practical terms all outdoor buildings should be waterproof and built on a solid foundation. The aspect is a major consideration; most summer houses are built in a sunny part of the garden to provide shade in the heat of summer. Ventilation is important as well, particularly if there is a lot of glass: this could be provided by windows that open or screens that slide. In exposed areas the walls of the building must protect people from the prevailing wind. In hot conditions there will be a need for blinds both to cool and to shade the building; they could have timber or aluminium slats resembling the linear patterns of Venetian blinds. For a softer look, threaded reed matting, machined split-bamboo canes or stiffened cotton fabric are all effective. They can be controlled by winding or pulling, using rolling or concertina folding.

Traditionally, summer houses were made of hardwoods like Western red cedar, Douglas fir, cedar or oak. Pressure-treated softwoods can be relatively durable, particularly if they are coated by protective paints or microporous timber stains formulated for external use. But the frame could equally be metal, steel or aluminium and the walls made of toughened, tinted, etched or transparent glass. New, ultraviolet-resistant plastics like polycarbonate sheeting also make translucent or opaque windows or walls. If these are hinged or removable, the building could have a completely open aspect in very hot weather.

For a contemporary look, the roof of a summer house may be clad with turf. These work best if pitched but are also effective when flat. In an austere, modern setting the look of a turf roof is surprising but very attractive. The existing roof needs a padded base over which you lay a waterproof layer of tough plastic sheeting, followed by the planting medium which may include rockwool or a lightweight compost. Lay the turf and make provision for drip irrigation, concealing the tubes behind the building. A turf roof is extremely easy to maintain by removing invasive weeds once or twice a year and trimming the grass with shears. An incidental virtue is that the summer house will have both thermal and sound insulation.

47

right *This intriguing summer house has a distinctly 'arts and crafts' look, but its steep, lightweight roof is made of self-bonded fibreglass that resembles lead.*

far right *Here a shade house is made from sturdy close-meshed hardwood trellis that filters strong sunlight. White-flowered* Clematis terniflora *rambles over the roof.*

This garden of considerable imagination, designed by Vladimir Sitta, uses quality materials like brass, which moves slightly when trodden on, for the walkway up to the entrance. Only a few centimetres above water level, it may be flooded so the path vanishes. The pool is lined with black granite and the aquatic plants are in copper containers. The oriental mood is echoed by arching bamboo.

water

Water is a wonderful means of expressing the spirit of the garden. It has always had an important role, from the Mogul gardens, the Persian paradise, then Spain and the extravagant water gardens of neo-classical Italy. In contemporary terms water is as important as it always has been, but with the emphasis now on simplicity. Modern gardens celebrate the qualities of water without the distraction of details and grandeur that had crept in over the centuries, with tiered fountains and spouting lion heads. Water today may be a gentle flow that barely breaks the surface or a silent, still depth which reflects the light of the sky; it may be a forceful spurt or merely a gentle dripping on to a mossy mound.

All aspects of the performance of water are explored in contemporary gardens: its transparency; its movement; its stillness; its noise; its silence; its power. It can be reduced to tiny droplets and may even be used to create water vapour, concealing mists through which we may wander. Much of this was unachievable in the past, but today we have techniques that can be controlled by electrical power. But creating such effects requires skill – the volume, speed, weight and power of water need to be understood and the plan carried out to appear totally effortless.

still water

Still water brings light from the sky to ground level; reflected clouds drift across, trees flicker and the ground becomes animated. Formal geometry generally means pools that are rectilinear, circular, polygonal or L-shaped, but in the contemporary garden attention is focused on the water's surface or its tranquil depths, as opposed to the pool's construction or decoration. Long strips of water such as rills, lying in parallel or at right angles to the associated building, enhance the tranquillity of a formal space. To integrate still water seamlessly within a courtyard, the paving

right *Water rises from a square pit and slides down into the shallow pool. Reflected in the water are the silver birch trunk and slim perspex water tube, animated by rising bubbles of air.*

far right *Designed by Topher Delaney, this shallow pool has a grid-like pattern of square concrete planters holding arum lilies (Zantedeschia aethiopica), surrounded with a 'mulch' of white cobbles. On the wall, slim stainless steel poles support climbers.*

may simply abut the pool, making an edge unnecessary. Or just a slight overhang may create a narrow, dark recess around the pool, leaving the high water surface almost level with the paving, without the interruption of a frame.

To keep a still pool free of algae, the water depth must be at least 45cm (18in). While still water should not be agitated, it must be aerated from time to time to keep it clean; installing a suitably sized pump would provide a means of circulating the water occasionally. Filters can also help to keep the water clean, while oxygenating plants (see apage 50) help to maintain its clarity. If there is too much continuous sunlight, you will have to consider the repeated use of algicides or cover part of the surface with suitable plants. Water lilies (*Nymphaea*) are best for still pools: their flat leaf discs break up the reflections, blending with modern simplicity.

There are some large-leaved water lilies, both hardy and tropical, as well as tiny 'pygmy' forms. The flowers, slightly raised above water level, come in white as well as ranges of yellow, pink and deep red; some flowers are deeply cupped, while others are distinctly starry. Choose your cultivar with care, according to its hardiness as well as to the size and depth of the pool.

far left *Curtains of fine nylon mesh part to lead into a circular enclosure. They are coated by water permeating from the pierced scaffolding above, creating a gauzy screen.*

left *Water bubbles through the drilled core of a water feature, made from smooth, precision-cut sandstone pillars, to slide down to the pebble-covered reservoir below.*

5 0   moving water

Movement does not have to mean agitation. A pool that brims over so that water slides into a gulley is ideal for the contemporary formal garden and a smooth, slow flow is gently suggestive of time passing. Water can possess the viscous character of oil, seductively sliding away with only a surface leaf to show that nothing stays quite the same. Slow-moving water features, often raised to hand height, are frequently used in minimalist gardens. The sculptor Luis Barragan revealed the simple elegance of such schemes in some of his Mexican courtyards.

The heavy nature of moving water may be exploited in different ways to create a dramatic scheme. When water is on the move, it froths and foams and fans and such rushing volume awakens the spirit, as at the famed water garden of the Villa d'Este, north of Rome, a maze of fantasy water effects with falls pounding disruptively on the stone below. A continuous roar can be wearing in today's smaller, more tranquil gardens and there may at times be need to return to a gentle splash. Fortunately, we have electrical power to control such agitation, so theatrical effects may be planned on a timer to be controlled by a switch.

There is a wider range of plants suited to moving water but in the formal garden it is best to stick to one or two – the aim is not to suggest a wild pool. The depth of planting is important and you need to think of this at the planning stage, before a pool is installed. Shelves should be built on which to place growing baskets, which are 10–20cm (4–8in) deep. Water plants are sold with a recommended depth of water above the soil, so the shelves must be deep enough to support basket and plant at its advised depth. If in doubt, allow for deeper shelves, as the plant height can be raised using a stone or brick block.

Edging plants or 'marginals' can be planted directly in very shallow water (2.5–7cm/1–3in). White kingcups (*Caltha palustris* var. *alba*) are an example, spreading well in damp soil at the edge of the pool or in only 2.5cm (1in) of water (that is, with the top of the basket 2.5cm/1in below water level). *Houttuynia cordata* 'Flore Pleno', with its blue-green, heart-shaped foliage, is another, requiring only 5–10cm (2–4in) of water. And the accommodating 80cm (2ft 8in) spear-shaped flag iris (*Iris pseudacorus*) can grow in moist soil no deeper than 15cm (6in). The water irises look particularly good in modern formal gardens because of their foliage and elegant flowers. Below the water surface, oxygenating plants like Canadian pondweed (*Elodea canadensis*) or, for summer, curled pondweed (*Potamogeton crispus*), help to keep moving pools clean; they will need lifting and splitting before they become invasive.

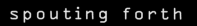

spouting forth

The static nature of modern formal gardens can be vividly brought to life by electrically controlled spurts of water. Here, it spills in a series of arcs from asymmetrically placed wall spouts to pour into a narrow canal adjacent to a swimming pool in this Caribbean garden. Clumps of papyrus and iris break the horizontal lines of the spare, modern design.

*A bridge follows an indirect route to encourage exploration of the water
surface and its floating lily pads, taking a line reminiscent of Japanese
zigzag bridges that were designed to ward off evil spirits. The concrete
surface has the soft, insubstantial look of a watercolour painting or
bronze verdigris.*

small water features

In modern small gardens pumped, recycled water may be ejected from chutes, sometimes overhead, or may slide smoothly down glass panels or emerge as a weir through a slit in the wall. It may follow the form of sheet metal, like satin-finish stainless steel, which contrasts with the polished transparency of the sheet of water, or deliberately oxidizing copper to create jade-green verdigris. Sometimes there is a swirling vortex where water is swallowed down through the central hole of a concrete disc, its effect utterly mesmerizing. Water may also be controlled to drip through a succession of containers, silently settling in a small pool below. With almost minimalist formality it may glide over a Perspex overhang, making a smooth, transparent weir. Computer-controlled jets of water, issuing from a grid of holes in the ground, have been used to create a three-dimensional, constantly changing water sculpture. The options are now limitless.

Electric pumps will circulate water and may be hidden within the design – behind a wall or sculpture, for example – or a submersible pump may be placed in the water. Both will need cleaning once a year. The size and type of pump will depend upon the volume of water and what is expected of it. Pumps may be operated from the mains or via a transformer, and it is advisable to have a circuit breaker fitted. Choosing the right pump and making the system operational is a skilled job and it is advisable to seek the help of an expert, who will make fine adjustments to the volume or character of the fountains or sprays on site.

right above *A chute pours into a shallow water trough, its floor covered with smooth, flat pebbles. These are echoed by the mosaic pattern of pebbles texturing the surrounding area.*

right *Water jets of varying height leap up from a grid of holes in the ground at Le Jardin de L'Imaginaire in Terrasson, France. The slim jets produce fine sprays that animate and freshen the garden.*

The galvanized metal cube holding the cardoon (Cynara cardunculus) has a sculptural presence on this roof garden made from modern materials, designed by Paul Thompson. The tall, branching perennial holds aloft large thistle-like magenta flowers in summer and its architectural grey spiny foliage blends well with the silvery metals.

sculpture & containers

right *Inviting disbelief, this suspended clay 'pod' appears to have produced a tree (in fact a small citrus) that forces its way through a crack.*

far right *Repetition suits the modern formal garden well. In this design by Topher Delaney flat uplighters, set in the concrete shelf, alternate with regimented clipped box in concrete containers and throw subtle shadows on to the smooth wall.*

When used as the focal point of the contemporary garden, sculpture should work in with its overall character. Either the material will blend or there will be a thought-provoking contrast. Modern sculpture may be figurative or abstract but in today's formal garden it is important to avoid reproduction pieces from a previous age, unless there is witty intent. The same applies to containers: however attractive a group of exuberantly planted pots is, the informal result will not suit the crisply styled contemporary garden. Far better to site identically planted pots symmetrically in pairs, in a line or in a formal group balanced by the harmony of an open space.

containers

Depending on their intended role, containers may be chosen to blend with or modestly ornament the site, or to have dramatic impact as a sculptural feature. Rectangular stone or concrete planters can be built in as part of the three-dimensional design. Or try duplicating much smaller, identical containers – say, timber cubes, cleanly shaped ceramic pots or galvanized metal planters – in rows that fall into line with the geometry of the plan. These could be planted with clipped box, myrtle or lavender, or a regiment of the slimly vertical grass *Calamagrostis* x *acutiflora*

'Stricta' or tufted hair grass (*Deschampsia caespitosa* 'Goldtau'). Echoing classical ideas, another effective way of presenting containers is to use them on the intersections of a grid, holding identical plants such as standard marguerites (*Argyranthemum frutescens*).

When planting containers for a formal garden, a single 'important' planter may hold one fine specimen like *Pinus mugo* or *Prunus glandulosa* 'Rosea Plena', both of which have a stylish profile all year. Alternatively, modern formality is well served by exotics like the fan palm (*Chamaerops humilis*), a flowering oleander (*Nerium*) or a lollipop-shaped citrus tree. Using an acidic compost would open up the possibilities of small azaleas that may be pruned to graceful shapes as done in Japan. Though flowering only once, these small evergreens have a charming presence. Placed as a dominant focal point, a single oversized container, made from terracotta or cold-cast 'lead' (bonded glass fibre), will emphasize scale and make enough impact without a plant. Avoid all container plants that have no definite shape: colour and prettiness will not do here. But silver foliage, like that of santolina and artemisia, as well as variegated irises and *Sisyrinchium striatum* will enhance a simple, spare scheme in sun.

All containers need watering, either by hand or as part of the installed irrigation scheme. Good drainage is important too and best achieved by placing a layer of broken crocks at the base of the pot. Always choose a compost made for container plants; a gritty compost will ensure adequate aeration. There are water-retaining polymer gels, sold in crystal form, that are mixed in with the compost to help hold water in a pot. Depending on its placement in the garden, the container may be fully exposed to sun or in full or partial shade – make your choice of plants accordingly.

sculpture

The materials used in modern sculpture range widely, from cast metals and glass fibre to frostproof ceramic pieces, carved stone and undressed stone. Concrete constructions and casts can be specially commissioned for the site. Metals may be immaculately polished or verdigris-ed with age, or colour may be present in painted resin-bonded materials or timber-built constructions.

Siting sculptural pieces needs thoughtful planning. This may be the only feature or the most dominant in the whole garden. Consider – is the work to be seen from inside or only outside? Is it freestanding or wall-mounted? A well-formed sculpture may need strong daylight, or its character may suggest a gentle, dappled light, inviting closer inspection. Will night lighting be important? If it is to be seen from the house, a tentative work will not do: clarity is all. If the piece is not monumentally important, several discreetly sited, more spiritual pieces can give enormous pleasure in a large garden when they are hidden from initial view and

'happened upon' in an area where the atmosphere is still and meditative. Some plants have a naturally sculptural form (see page 70) and should not be overlooked when thinking of a focal point. Trees are obvious candidates: a single frangipani (*Plumeria*) would be wonderful in a warm climate. Smaller trees like Japanese acers are elegant even in winter, while the winter-flowering mahonias, like the erect *M. lomariifolia* which can grow to 3m (10ft), have dramatically sculpted, long spiny leaves as well as upright racemes of fragrant yellow flowers.

found objects

If economy is relevant, *objets trouvés* of an organic nature, like contorted weathered tree roots, timbers bleached by the sea, flint piles, a single rock or boulder or a group of three in Japanese style, will all bring a sculptural presence. In the oriental garden objects are perceived to have a spirit power of the natural world, symbolized here by the choice of natural object. An effective asymmetric group might include one erect rock, one flat rock and an upturned dead tree root, arms akimbo to the sky. Even man-made items, like buoys and floats, an industrial machine relic or architectural salvage, can be entertaining, but avoid a casual display or a sense of clutter: one or three is enough. Make more of the piece by siting it on a plinth or alone in a clear, empty space – it then acquires the status of art. The aim of the modern garden is simple formality, not a distracting mish-mash of memorabilia, however charming.

opposite far left *Making a strongly sculptural statement, the oversized brick arch indicates a transition from formal garden to kitchen garden.*

opposite centre *Straggling spiny* Euphorbia milii *var.* splendens *grows from a tall concave clay container whose sculptural shape is set against a terracotta-washed wall.*

opposite left *A concrete monument by Topher Delaney stands sentinel against a rural backdrop; there is a viewing slit down the centre.*

House 'walls' made from sliding window panels wrap around three sides of a simple courtyard, designed by the author, with the solid fourth wall of brick. The only light comes from above, limiting the planting prospects to ferns, bamboo and ivy. The painted timber sculpture stands in for plant vitality because it changes with the light, suggesting perpetual movement.

This superb wood-floored roof terrace, enclosed by white rendered walls and a high slatted timber trellis, is softly lit at night. The hidden light sources create a gentle glow and light is reflected off the underside of the canvas awning.

lighting

At night gardens are transformed by subtle lighting and may take on a new persona. Evening fragrances draw us outside and the scented night garden, once thought of as a luxury, is becoming an essential ingredient of outdoor life. Technology has advanced so far that lighting is now safe, controllable and can create a nightscape that may be as theatrical as the owner chooses. This is particularly appropriate for the urban garden which is continuously on view from the house.

The effects created by lighting are interchangeable and variable. Tall trees may be uplit by a concealed spotlight at ground level: there is nothing more magnificent than the structure of an Atlantic cedar revealed against the black velvet night. Or trees may have soft lights concealed among their branches and angled downwards, providing a terrace with enough light to dine by. For accent, a small spot of light may focus upon a water feature, sculpture, container or special plant and backlit plants silhouetted on plain walls are always dramatic. A different spirit is created when a gentle wash of light spreads in front of foliage, creating flickering moving shadows. And a fascinating mirror effect is achieved by putting a hidden light source at the far end of a still pool to light trees above, their beauty then reflected in the black pool.

Safety is as important as function in the night garden but, provided this is met, there is no need for the light source to be glaringly obvious. Steps, paths, water, low hedges and other hazards can be successfully lit by concealed downlighting. But there are some stylish contemporary lights which it would be a crime not to reveal. Glowing slim opaque wands, erectly grouped among herbaceous plants, are elegantly suited to modern simplicity. Certain 'hatted' lights spread a circle of light beneath them, revealing beautifully crafted paving detail without emitting any glare, and some linear wall fixtures create rhythmical patterns of light.

5 8

illuminated water troughs

The magnificent modern 'paradise' garden designed by Martha Schwartz is based on a formal grid pattern, with slim water channels connecting one square brick platform to another. Every rill is edged with strongly coloured tiles and inside each brick plinth is a sunken cube of space for a slim fountain. These recessed pits are illuminated by a hidden light that also emphasizes the fountain. Coarse white rocks fill the square areas around ornamental *Malus*.

installing lighting

New lighting techniques are based on the use of transformers that convert domestic power to low voltage. The power is reduced, making it far safer to use outside. From the mains cable loop ringing the garden, another low-voltage cable runs several lights. If too many lights are used, or the secondary cable is too long, the strength of the light is reduced. The advantages of this are that the lights themselves may be smaller and therefore less visible in daylight and the bulbs last longer. Some modern lights have their own transformer fitted; these are more powerful and ideal for spotlighting large trees.

Inexpensive systems are available where the lights can be moved around the garden, but it is vital to employ a skilled professional to install these. A qualified approved electrician will advise on a system suited to your space, knowing the power and quality of the lights available as well as how to place lights under water, in a pool or beneath a weir. He will put in a residual circuit breaker and can plan the system so that it is operated from within the house – added to which he will have insurance against accident, which you may not.

lanterns

Not all night lighting need be powered electrically. The simplicity of flickering candlelight is superbly moody in the night garden but of course the slightest breeze puts you in the dark again. However, there are now cheap, very pretty candle holders that protect the flame with simple glass tubing or a glass cover that slides into place as wanted. Some of these lanterns may hang from tall slim lightweight aluminium spikes with a large hook on one end, rather like a shepherd's crook. From these spikes, many different types of lantern can be suspended at a chosen height,

opposite *A line of stylish wall-mounted lights illuminate the steps at night and make a feature of the silhouetted spiralled handrail in this garden by Martha Schwartz.*

far left *The simplest lighting is often the most effective. Here, the small granite monolith provides an elemental shelf for a candle.*

left *Uplighters draw attention to the elegant habit of shapely plants such as the fig tree (Ficus elastica) and the traveller's palm (Ravenala madagascariensis), at either end of a swimming pool.*

singly, in pairs or massed for effect. The same lights can be suspended from trees to glow for many hours. Glass protectors may be coloured but in the formal garden you should avoid a technicolor effect. A mass of small blue glass containers filled with small night lights would illuminate the darkened garden with great moonlit charm, but warm natural flames take some beating behind plain glass. Restraint is always the key in a formal setting.

Old-fashioned oil lamps are enjoying a revival, as are natural flame torches, but both sources of light must be treated with respect as they are potentially hazardous. The light source itself may be hidden for safety as well as effect behind a mesh screen where no one will go. Above all, do not pollute the modern garden with light. Keep the aims simple: too much jewellery spoils the dress and the same applies to lighting the night garden.

Formality offers today's gardener a good starting point, a way to bring some order to the natural exuberance of foliage and flowers. Traditionally, when gardens were planned formally, the plants chosen were those best suited to a geometric layout, either because they had natural form or could have a distinct shape imposed upon them. Pencil-slim Italian cypresses, as seen in the great Italian gardens, and familiar low hedges of clipped box fitted in with the geometry extremely well.

The same plant material is still appropriate but today's less restricted palette includes many other plants equally suited to contemporary interpretations of formality. These include several small-foliaged shrubs that, like box, can be sheared to shape. But modern ideas of formality can also be served by including plants with dramatic architectural form, those with huge leaves and exotic-looking species that add a new twist to schemes. Trees, too, have a major role in the modern classic garden. A sequence of trees may line a route or a pair flank an entrance as part of the arranged order, whereas a single tree can play a soloist role in a pared-down garden.

plants

No tree is more elegant than the Japanese acer, here doubly celebrated in shadowy form against a plain wall.

below *These immaculately clipped box hedges have a rounded form, rather than the usual sharply defined rectangular shape. The sinuous green enclosures are filled variously with velvety grass, small topiary mounds and single trees.*

clippable plants

Strong lines and shapes can be made by adjusting a plant's natural growth habit and formal gardens have always relied heavily on the clipped forms of evergreens such as box (Buxus sempervirens) and yew (*Taxus baccata*). Other accommodating evergreen shrubs, like myrtle (*Myrtus communis*) and cotton lavender (*Santolina chamaecyparissus*) are ideal for precision shaping because they have dense, small-foliaged growth that regenerates from the stems or branches. When sheared, the mass of tiny leaves makes it easy to achieve sharp edges. Even when the profile is blurred by new growth, the density of these shrubs ensures the maintenance of the form.

64

hedges and parterres

Hedging can be the most influential element in a formal garden. The architectural nature of continuous runs of hedging may be used to emphasize a geometric layout, define routes and vistas, add boundaries and enclose spaces. Whether it is as tall as a two-storey house or as short as 15cm (6in), an evergreen hedge is constant in winter and a good backdrop in summer. Parterres traditonally made patterns in the garden. They developed from the idea of using low hedges to define and edge small beds, usually of geometric design, filled with low-growing herbs like thymes. As the fashion evolved, parterre designs became more elaborate, sometimes taking the shape of a fleur-de-lys or a swirl of paisley, and the spaces were filled with seasonal flowers or simply coloured gravels.

hedges

Yew is the richest backcloth for any garden. It is dark and classy and will do as well in shade as in sunlight. It is renowned for its longevity and, because new leaves will grow even from very old tree trunks, it can

A garden is whimsically peopled with abstract topiary, tightly controlled but asymmetrically placed. The 'crowds' have parted to leave a circular green path that leads directly to a straight one beyond.

opposite below *The pleached beech stilt hedge formally defines and encloses part of the garden, designed by David Hicks. In place of a view through, the tree trunks make a vertical repeat pattern against a backing of more clipped beech.*

always be relied upon to renew the form required. Where winter temperatures drop well below freezing, the European yew (*Taxus baccata*) will not do and should be replaced by *Taxus* x *media* 'Brownii'. This has a slightly softer look, yet can be clipped with the same sharp accuracy. All yews will suffer in poorly drained soil, needing it to be moist but free-draining as well as acid to neutral. When well suited, yews will grow as much as 30cm (12in) in a year; they should be clipped only once, in mid- to late summer. Yews are toxic so should not be planted adjacent to meadows because of the risk to domestic animals.

Other conifers, like *Thuja plicata* 'Atrovirens', create dense, lighter green hedging with a softer look. And for the fastest grower in the west, Lawson's cypress (*Chamaecyparis lawsoniana*) grows at a rate of 1m (3ft 3in) a year. Like all forest trees, these conifers should be clipped, early in their life, to approximately 30cm (12in) below the chosen height so that the softer growth will thicken before attaining full height the following

year. After this, an annual clipping regime is essential to maintain a dense hedge; avoid cutting into the old wood, however.

Large-leaved hedges like hornbeam (*Carpinus betulus*), elaeagnus, laurel (*Prunus laurocerasus*) and beech (*Fagus sylvatica*) may be used in the formal garden where they will give a softer profile than more tightly shaped plants. They can be clipped but look better when cut by hand with secateurs. Both deciduous hornbeam and lime (*Tilia*) may be pleached, which involves training their side branches horizontally to create parallel lines, to develop a stilt hedge. In this procedure, all other growth is woven in or removed, forming a dense leafy screen for 1.5–2m (5ft–6ft 6in) above the row of tree trunks, 1.5m (5ft) in height, which allow low views through. Stilt hedges are best purchased pre-formed, with their parallel lateral branches already trained to a timber frame. A revival of old techniques includes the use of woven and clipped hazel and willow hedges in contemporary gardens; they can be ordered ready-trained.

far left *In a design by Christopher Bradley-Hole, a terracotta-washed rendered wall backs a raised brick planting bed. The materials are traditional but the uncompromising precision and simplicity are not.*

left *This modern garden has all the ingredients of traditional formality: yew hedges, box-edged beds and topiary. Yew cones in the centre of the lavender-filled parterres wittily echo the white obelisks designed by George Carter.*

66 dwarf hedges and parterres

There are many different forms of common box (*Buxus sempervirens*) that will reach over 6m (20ft) high and wide if required. But the slower-growing dwarf version, *B. sempervirens* 'Suffruticosa', which may grow to 1.2m (4ft), can support really meticulous clipping to maintain a medium or low edging hedge of 75cm (2ft 6in) down to 30cm (12in). It is perfect for preserving the detail of parterres. There is a variegated form, *B. sempervirens* 'Elegantissima', with cream edging. The Japanese box (*B. microphylla*) has tiny leaves and the form 'Green Pillow' makes squat hummocks which look stylish in a minimalist group or repeat planted.

Other hardy plants suited to low sheared hedging and therefore often used to build parterres include some with silver-grey foliage. Cotton lavender (*Santolina*), cultivars of scented lavender like *Lavandula angustifolia* 'Hidcote' and the tender French lavender (*L. stoechas*) will provide gentle grey dwarf hedges. Both the clippable evergreens *Lonicera nitida* and *L. pileata* have tiny green leaves. In a warm, sunny climate, the aromatic but slightly tender myrtle can take over from box. It grows fast and can be clipped low or at 2.5m (8ft) if needed. Look for the subspecies *tarentina*, the most compact and windproof, which was a favourite in Roman gardens and is still popular in Mediterranean regions today.

topiary

Topiary is an ancient craft in which suitable evergreen plants are tightly clipped to shape to make freestanding sculptural forms. All the small-leaved evergreens referred to above, particularly box and yew, as well as hollies and the reliable but rather dull privet (*Ligustrum*) can be clipped into any chosen shape. Though hollies will lose their crop of berries when sculpted, the foliage has a coarse-textured look, emphasized when variegated, and this can enliven a topiary garden of yew and box. The sculptural possibilities of these plants have historically been explored as spirals, cones, pyramids and layered 'cakestands', as well as the whimsy of animals and grotesques. These have now largely given way to the more minimalist geometry of cubes, cylinders, rectangles or Art Deco shapes.

Topiary work imparts a silent presence to the garden, instilling respect for the space and bringing the visitor to a halt. In the past, it was used formally to mark entrances, flank paths and add year-round ornamental form, emphasizing a garden's three-dimensional design by its static presence. Today topiary is still used for the same purposes but in a far less ornamental manner, while its abstract, creative impact has come to the fore. These stationary sculptures are often placed so that they produce an asymmetric tension, emphasizing the space around them. And while

cubist hedges

The effect of this large, contemporary plot, set against light woodland, is tranquil, formal and pleasing.
Designer Piet Blanckaert has used strictly geometric shapes of cubes, pillars and wide rectangles to set out an
interesting yet asymmetric layout that invites inspection across a timber bridge over the 'canal'. To the right
is an elaborate modern parterre, its box-edged swirls left empty and itself enclosed by a low hedge. Massed
rhododendrons provide a transition between the two areas.

top *A path is flanked by small standards of clipped box, growing from massed* Lavandula angustifolia *'Twickel Purple', both classic ingredients of formal gardens.*

above *In this narrow, Japanese-inspired courtyard by Luciano Giubbilei the focal point is a well-sculpted 'cloud topiary' of box. The still pool is made from glass bricks.*

geometric forms like pyramids, cones and spires take the eye upwards, rounded forms squat together, making small mountainous hillocks.

Ancient topiary has often lost its original precision and new shapes have developed over the centuries, the living result a happy compromise between man and nature. These abstract shapes are neither symmetrical, geometric nor figurative but instead have become strangely deformed 'mounds' with a theatrical presence. The formality of oriental topiary is a little like this; it is less mathematical and more organic, taking the plant's growth habit into account. In the gardens of Japan, azaleas are often topiaried to make compact mounds. Their small, densely packed leaves cope well with hard pruning so they can be shaped into almost any form but are usually clipped as rounded hillocks, crammed together like boulders or clouds. Azaleas tolerate being annually restrained so that they remain the same size, which is part of the reassuring tranquillity of the garden. However, the seasons change their appearance and since azaleas flower it is best they are one colour: a patchwork would disrupt the calm.

An oriental influence can also be a softening one in modern classic gardens. 'Cloud' topiary is moulded from the natural habit of a shrub by selecting wide-spreading branches to hold out small cumulus mounds of clipped foliage; all non-essential branches are removed. Box, holly (*Ilex crenata*), *Juniperus chinensis* and pines like Japanese white pine (*Pinus parviflora*) are suitable; a pretty Chinese privet (*Ligustrum lucidum*), often available as a small lollipop tree, can also be clipped as cloud topiary.

practicalities When clipping topiary, assess right angles using a plumb-line, or make a wooden frame or template to use every year. 'Formers' can be purchased ready-made in wood or metal and these are retained within the finished work, rather like armatures. Yew needs clipping once a year and box and lonicera twice. Faster-growing shrubs like privet demand regular attention every two to three weeks. Hand shears will enable you to keep control of any freestanding shape, whereas electric shears are ideal for long runs of hedging and will maintain the precision of established large topiary. The sides of tall hedging should be battered towards the top, allowing light to reach the lower areas and snow to slide off the hedge. Some specialists will carry out bespoke topiary if you are not confident about doing it yourself; once shaped, however, both hedges and topiary are simple to maintain.

George Carter designed this superbly elegant formal garden, using parallel strips of still water and pale, loose-laid gravel. A grid of London plane trees rises from formal 'plinths' of clipped box. The boundary beyond is made of slim timber trellis, painted grey and backed by galvanized sheet metal that brings luminosity to the garden.

architectural & exotic

Modern formality may be orderly but it is certainly not predictable. One of the charms of today's designs is that there are fewer preconceptions as to how a garden should look, so native plants with strong form as well as exotic-looking subjects from sub-tropical climates are frequently included in the layout to add an element of surprise and challenge. You may need to choose a reliably hardy form for a protected environment or use more tender species in containers that are brought outdoors only for the summer. Check with a local nursery if in any doubt about a plant's suitability for your climate.

Architectural and exotic plants can be used singly, or they may be planted in linear regiments or as a group. Used as soloists, they draw the eye and could be the focus of a minimalist garden. They may emphasize layout by being planted in lines, while in a group they can add drama to an otherwise humdrum, easily maintained geometric background.

architectural plants

The all-important atmosphere of a garden is greatly affected by the types of plant selected, and plant form speaks volumes in a formal setting. Those plants that grow naturally with a clear outline create shapes and silhouettes which have great character; naturally large-leaved examples include the frost-tender silvery *Melianthus major* for sun and rodgersias for shade. Where there is a lot of detail in a garden, these shapes help to establish a focus which draws the eye.

The shape of a plant often determines how we use it; its inherent formality may be exact and geometric, as in the Irish juniper (*Juniperus communis* 'Hibernica'), or studiedly asymmetrical, as in the best forms of Japanese maple (*Acer*). Vertical outlines catch the eye whichever purpose they serve and sword-like foliage is just as focused. Stiff sword-like shapes

such as that of New Zealand flax (*Phormium tenax*) will always stand out. The sword leaves grow from the base of this plant, fanning out widely, so it needs space. In its native country, the smooth grey leaves with tall panicles of dark plum-red flowers reach 3m (10ft). It benefits from a mild climate, where it will reach its natural ultimate height, but when less well suited the height may be reduced to about 1.8m (6ft). There are also variegated and reddish forms, as well as some smaller cultivars like the brown-red *P.* 'Bronze Baby' which is only 45–60cm (18–24in). Because of their uncompromising structure, all phormiums suit formal gardens. Among the smaller *P. cookianum* cultivars there are some, like the 1.5m (5ft) tall *P. cookianum* subsp. *hookeri* 'Cream Delight', whose reflexed outer leaves shine in the light, creating a softer look.

Some crocosmias and flag irises have similarly tall, elegant, lanceolate foliage with knife-points, but they are deciduous and their bright green colouring has a less dramatic effect than the grey-greens and purples of the phormiums, so they merge rather easily with other plant leaves.

foliage plants for shade

Formality in the shaded garden can be achieved using a framework of clipped shrubs with some audaciously large-leaved plants. Shapely foliage is an asset, particularly when it is evergreen. Architects choosing to flatter their town houses often use the easy-going evergreen shrub *Fatsia japonica* and its variegated form *F. japonica* 'Variegata' (both 1.5–4m/ 5–12ft), because they have large, glossy, palmate leaves that look good against walls even in dense shade. The admirable acanthus also earned respect from architects a long time ago, in ancient Greece, as can be seen on the capitals of Corinthian columns. The statuesque *Acanthus spinosus*, almost 1.5m (5ft) when its flower spikes are fully fledged, will do well in

left *Spikily etched against the sky, the Chusan palm (Trachycarpus fortunei), with its shaggy trunk, is beautifully displayed above a curved, cream wall.*

left below *Shallow cones of crushed glass, resembling rice, rise from a pool while a mulch of blue crushed glass covers beds in this extraordinary garden, planted with 'exotics' like bananas, agaves and aloes.*

light shade or full sun. Its deeply divided, sharply pointed foliage is magnificent but this plant must have space. These large-leaved plants make a strong statement wherever they are.

Most plants with large leaves are best suited to shaded, damp areas where the rate of evaporation from their leaves is slower. In temperate gardens rodgersias, rheums, cimicifugas and ligularias have great foliage presence; their large leaves are either rounded or jagged and they have tall flower spikes in summer. In the formal country garden, foxgloves (*Digitalis*) look good rising from groundcover comprising large hostas (like *H.* 'Big Daddy'), bergenias (like *B.* 'Ballawley') and the invasive, massive-leaved *Trachystemon orientalis*, all of which, with their overlapping leaves, create formal effects and can serve the need for low maintenance.

71

shapely plants for sun

For flowering as well as foliage interest in hot spots there are some rigidly erect herbaceous plants, like the brilliant columns of kniphofias, rising from knife-pointed leaves, or the huge foxtail lilies (*Eremurus robustus*) that grow vertically to a height of 2.5m (8ft) and more. Plants like these may be used in summer as sentinels, marking either side of an entrance, or will make a random Manhattan-like skyline of white, pink, cream or yellow. Other bold temperate plants with skyward ambitions include massive hybrid delphiniums, although these do need staking; some grow over 2.5m (8ft) and are a pathetic sight when snapped by the wind. The older Belladonna Hybrids are shorter, up to 1.5m (5ft), but they are similarly aspirant and produce successive spikes through to late autumn. All enjoy free-draining, neutral soil.

The sharp, silvery magnificence of the cardoon (*Cynara cardunculus*) requires sunlight and space to accommodate a circumference of 1.8m (6ft).

Macleaya microcarpa 'Kelway's Coral Plume' requires less space as it grows more vertically, attaining 2.1m (7ft). The large lobed leaves are dove-grey with white undersides and the flowers are fluffily fine, contrasting with the smooth, flat leaves. This plume poppy is one of the few large-leaved plants that will grow in direct sunlight, apart from those sub-tropicals that live in high humidity; free-draining soil is important.

Two appropriate biennials should be mentioned here – one is the silver-grey, lethally spiny Scotch thistle (*Onopordum acanthium*), which grows to a height of 1.8m (6ft) by the second summer. The other, which has contrastingly luminous grey woolly leaves, is the giant mullein (*Verbascum olympicum*) which reaches over 2m (6ft 6in).

exotic plants

Contemporary designers of formal gardens often look to 'foreigners' to provide a dramatically different summer look and they experiment with these tender exotics to create a garden magnificently out of context with its surroundings. By 'exotics', I mean plants that have dramatic foliage and extravagant form. They usually come from sub-tropical parts of the world but can often be grown successfully in cooler climates given a sheltered, warm position where the soil is rich and will not dry out but drains freely. They are often faster-growing than the smaller-leaved plants native to temperate climates and can take over in a competitive situation.

This is not a modest or sentimental garden style – it is bold and exciting. In the modern garden these exotics can be ravishingly different, brilliantly coloured and powerfully foliaged. The hardiest ones, like the fan palm and dwarf fan palm (see opposite), will set the skeletal form of a scheme, used either as an individual focus or in regimented lines, like the orange trees of Versailles. More fragile specimens like daturas may then be slotted in for the summer season, provided they are grown in containers that can be taken back indoors for winter.

Some spiky-leaved yuccas are hardy, such as the trunkless *Yucca filamentosa*, surviving at temperatures of -10°C (14°F), but others are less so, like the neatly compact, stemless *Y. whipplei*, which should be grown only in the warmest areas and well protected, if necessary, from cold winter rain. And *Y. gloriosa*'s massive 60cm (2ft) long flower panicles carry creamy-white hanging bells over a trunk with dagger-like leaves. The magnificent grey lanceolate foliage of yuccas is not to be trifled

opposite *Against a background of stark modernity Isabelle Greene designed this drought-tolerant garden in California where agaves mix with aeoniums, yuccas with sedum, fescues with pennisetums, all set off by soft grey and green foliage.*

right *An urban setting is an unlikely place to find the tender blue fan palm (*Brahea armata*). Yet this garden, designed by Stephen Woodhams, is sufficiently sheltered to grow them in galvanized metal containers; they can be taken indoors for winter if frost threatens.*

far right *Grown in regimented lines, cannas have great formality and bring height and rich colour to a bed.*

with, so these are not plants for the family garden. A yucca-like plant, *Beschorneria yuccoides*, must be grown in a sunny position where it may bake in summer, but it needs some protection from wind, like a south-facing wall, and well-drained soil. Its red flower panicles are a rewarding sight. The spiked foliage of cordylines is less threatening but every bit as stylish. *Cordyline australis*, the hardiest species, survives at -5°C (23°F), grradually reaching over 15m (50ft), but also consider *C. indivisa*, with its large crown slowly growing to 3m (10ft) in warmer sites.

From the really arid areas of the world come the extraordinary shapes of cacti. These reservoirs of water grow into tough, distinctive fleshy forms. Most are unsuitable for transplanting but some of the prickly pears (*Opuntia*) from North America will adjust to growing in areas that are guaranteed frost-free. But unless you have really hot, dry conditions, the choices will be limited. In desert heat, wonderful shapes and colours are to be found, like the little rounded *Cereus* species and *Echinocactus*, contrasting with the prickly pears. They are in the colourful company of aloes, like the 2m (6ft 6in) tall, flowering *Aloe arborescens*, agaves like *Agave americana* 'Variegata', wickedly sharp and with a height and spread of 2m (6ft 6in), or aeoniums, such as *Aeonium arboreum* 'Magnificum', which is 60cm (2ft) tall but 1m (3ft 3in) wide, with frost-

hardy *Zauschneria californica* 'Glasnevin', a clumpy perennial with tubular scarlet flowers and spurges such as *Euphorbia seguieriana*, a bushy, frost-hardy plant of 45cm (18in) with glaucous foliage and terminal flowers that are acid-yellow.

Palms are classified as sword, feathered or fan, which is an indication of their distinctive shapes, but most suit only gardens where they are protected from frost by glass. The Chinese fan palm *Trachycarpus fortunei* will survive in mild areas if the temperature is no lower than -5°C (23°F); it has a tree-like habit, growing to about 8m (27ft), with 1m (3ft 3in) wide fans on every stem. *Chamaerops humilis*, the dwarf fan palm of 1.5m (5ft) height and spread, is ideal for smaller gardens; it is frost-tender, needing a minimum temperature of 7°C (45°F). Growing these palms alongside grey-foliaged plants and an evergreen *Euphorbia characias* subsp. *wulfenii*, with its branches of crowded narrow leaves forming a rounded shrub 1.2m (4ft) wide, makes for a Mediterranean style of formality.

More exotic foliage effects come from bamboos like *Phyllostachys nigra*, with ebony canes, growing to approximately 3.5m (11ft) in cooler climates or the huge *P. viridiglaucescens* (7.5m/25ft) which will survive at -20°C (-4°F). There are smaller ones like the pygmy bamboos that are

top *One of the tallest and slimmest of herbaceous perennials, the columnar foxtail lily (*Eremurus 'Romance'*) is an insistent eye-catcher.*

above *In the Huntington Botanical gardens, squat rounds of globe cacti (*Echinocactus grusonii*) catch the light; a tall* Trichocereus pasacana *stands sentinel among them, backed by exotic dracaenas and yuccas.*

good for neat edging but many are very invasive. Even in temperate climates you can have success with a banana (*Musa basjoo*), which needs a wide space to reveal its assets. It will not produce fruit, but the magnificent paddle-like leaves may be 1m (3ft 3in) long; provided it is wrapped in horticultural fleece for winter, the banana will ultimately reach 3–5m (10–15ft) with a diameter of 2–2.5m (6–8ft). And from Tasmania come the tree ferns (*Dicksonia antarctica*), with their low, wide canopy of fronds now being grown in surprisingly cool areas, though they are half-hardy to frost-tender and prefer humus-rich, moist soil. You can buy short trunks from the garden centre but eventually tree ferns grow to 10m (30ft) and, with their summer canopy, will be up to 4m (12ft).

Brilliant colour among exotics can be achieved with the flowering cannas from South America, crinums from tropical Asia, *Aloe aristata* and *Ricinus* from tropical Africa, daturas (*Brugmansia*) from the West Indies, *Eucomis* from South Africa and ginger lilies (*Hedychium*) from India. In temperate climates, these can be grown indoors and put out in summer where, among the more modestly coloured northern plants, they will stand out and instantly add drama to the garden (see page 154 for more ideas using striking exotics).

Consider the siting of exotics carefully, for example placing them in dappled light where necessary or against walls in full sun, but avoiding east-facing walls because the early morning sun will thaw frosted buds and flowers too quickly, 'burning' them brown. Be sure that the moisture level is constant or that free drainage is available as needed. Protection with horticultural fleece in winter will widen the scope of sub-tropical species that can remain outside or you could contemplate moving such plants indoors for winter if you have room. Straw, bracken or even old newspapers can also be used to protect tender plants; sacking or hessian strips will hold them in place but they will not be very attractive in winter. There are other methods of wind protection, such as setting out temporary screens of fine-mesh nylon netting or, more attractively, by installing woven hurdles of hazel or willow around the plants.

The magnificent biennial, silver-grey Onopordum acanthium, *with its striking outline, is planted to rise above a groundcover of yarrow and grass. While the plants are informal in character, the layout is based on a grid pattern and the planting backed by a clipped dark green hedge of yew.*

trees

In the traditional formal garden, trees made avenues, emphasizing vistas and framing the view. Sometimes they were wide-spreading, deciduous, broad-leaved trees, like beech, elm or chestnut. At other times, narrow trees like the Lombardy poplar (*Populus nigra* 'Italica') or Italian cypress (*Cupressus sempervirens* Stricta Group) created soaring lines flanking wide paths. On a smaller scale, limes were often pollarded, which involves training a single stem to be cut annually or biennially to a height of 1.8m (6ft) or more. The new growth will have particularly large leaves at accessible heights, bestowing shade. More recently, wider, arching trees like the flowering cherry (*Prunus serrulata* 'Longipes', syn. *P.* 'Shimizu-zakura') have made a low, flattened vault for the visitor to walk beneath and smaller trees like *Laburnum* x *watereri* 'Vossii' have been trained over a frame to make tunnels.

By planting trees in duplicate rows, symmetrical designs created strong axes in the larger garden. To ensure uniform 'avenues', the trees must be identical and chosen from vegetatively produced material – that is, cuttings – rather than seedlings that may grow at different rates or be mismatched in colour and habit. If your site is small you need not be without a tree. Consider the possibilities of a mini-woodland of three or five narrow trees, such as *Betula pendula* 'Tristis', planted as closely as 1m (3ft 3in) apart; they will ultimately reach a height of 15m (50ft). But the single tree has an important role as a focus. It could be linked with the ground by a low shrub or rocks, or stand as a soloist. It need not be placed in the middle of the garden space but would look better off-centre. Alternatively, the same tree could be twinned in a dynamic relationship diagonally across the area of a courtyard. Ideal trees for very restricted spaces include the slow-growing Japanese acers or the 5m (15ft) high *Sorbus vilmorinii*.

top *Cool grey-painted timber makes a raised dais that sets off the lime-washed tree trunks of pruned, dome-shaped* Malus 'Adams' *and emphasizes the formal layout of the garden.*

above *Two grafted weeping mulberry trees (*Morus alba 'Pendula'*), with lime-washed trunks, will stay small and can be pruned to shape.*

Betula pendula *'Tristis' is a narrow weeping tree that acts*
as a focal point in this restrained gravelled garden,
softening the severity of its plain cream walls.

Trees are invaluable because they give a sense of permanence and add a three-dimensional aspect – we literally look up to them. They may be selected for their changing seasonal performance or for striking foliage, but the main priority has to be their form, because this has a sculptural effect on the new formal garden scene.

form

Many trees are naturally well formed, lending themselves to the most rigorous geometry. They may be fastigiate – that is, columnar – or make wide-spreading arches, weeping mounds, or mopheads. Tall, vertical forms punch a hole in the horizon, so such specimens will act as a focus, like the wonderful 15m (50ft) incense cedars (*Calocedrus decurrens*) or huge 30m (100ft) *Ginkgo biloba* 'Fastigiata'. Slow growth can be expected from the cypress oak (*Quercus robur* 'Fastigiata') but it will in time produce a distinguished column up to 20m (65ft) tall. *Fagus sylvatica* 'Dawyck' will grow to make a narrow vertical of the same height.

For smaller spaces there are garden trees with the same vertical habit, like flowering cherries (*Prunus* 'Amanogawa' at 10m/30ft), crab apples (*Malus* 'Van Eseltine' at 6m/20ft) and rowans (*Sorbus aucuparia* 'Sheerwater Seedling' at 4m/12ft), as well as two pleasing maples, *Acer* 'Scanlon' and *A. saccharum* subsp. *nigrum* 'Temple's Upright'.

Mopheaded trees like the silvery weeping pear (*Pyrus salicifolia* 'Pendula') are attractive when spaced in ranks along a path. A darkly evergreen tree, the holm oak (*Quercus ilex*) has often been used formally as it is easily maintained in a tight, rounded form, but when not trained becomes a big tree 25m (80ft) high. Other round-headed trees like the mophead acacia (*Robinia pseudoacacia* 'Umbraculifera') lend themselves naturally to repetition, with a height and spread of 6m (20ft); they look

lonely when isolated, unless the garden is small. Avoid windy sites because the branches are brittle. Many hollies are naturally round-headed as well as some of the thorns, like *Crataegus pedicellata* at 5m (15ft).

flower and fruit

Flowering trees have extra seasonal value, enlivening the formal picture with their blossoms or fruits. As well as the popular cherries and crab apples, both the rowan and hawthorn have come to the fore. Rowans often have two seasons of charm – spring flowers and autumn fruiting. Among the rowans, the small *Sorbus cashmiriana*, only 9m (30ft) tall, has a domed form with feathery foliage and trusses of white spring flowers, followed by clusters of white berries. The taller *S. hupehensis* has a more erect character and also carries drooping clusters of white fruit. There are red-, orange- and yellow-berried forms of rowan but the very small *S. vilmorinii* (5m/15ft) has pink fruits and elegantly delicate foliage.

Hawthorns are made of sterner stuff, having a more rigid habit. Until recently they have been rather overlooked in favour of cherries and crab apples, but a reliable form like *Crataegus laevigata* 'Paul's Scarlet' (6m/20ft) is very hardy and will survive in wet clay. I particularly like a hawthorn often used as a street tree, *C. persimilis* 'Prunifolia' (8m/27ft): it is firmly rounded and has rich red autumn colour and glowing scarlet fruits. These trees of rather strict habit are ideal grown in rows or grid patterns; they lack the elegance of single specimen trees like acers.

canopies

Light is such an important part of all gardens that it must be borne in mind when choosing trees, even though the profile created by the tree's shape is the priority in many formal gardens. For example, light will not

serene symmetry

In a garden designed by David Hicks, this wonderful symmetrical vista, luminous in frosty winter light, derives its impact from the planting of horse chestnut trees. The avenues lining it are reminiscent of the long allées of the past in which the axis would traditionally have culminated in a temple or classical sculpture. Here, the wide mown path leads through three set stages, starting with the reflective surface of a still, geometric pool and ending at a cleft in the horizon.

Autumnal changes bring warmth to a formally planned garden. Liquidambar styraciflua has beautifully delineated leaves that colour magnificently.

come through trees with dense canopies, like the hawthorns. The canopy of the widely spreading Indian bean tree (*Catalpa bignonioides*), 10m (33ft) in height and spread, also creates dense shade beneath due to its hugely wide leaves. Large pinnate foliage like that of the Japanese angelica tree (*Aralia elata*), which has the same dimensions, hides the light from plants below, but this is a pretty tree with architectural shape and large creamy flower panicles; there is an attractive variegated form. A dense canopy is also characteristic of the evergreen loquat (*Eriobotrya japonica*), a frost-hardy tree which does best in a warm, protected site. This too has a spreading form but is small enough to be grown as a shrub, or clipped to a neater shape growing up to 8m (27ft).

But light filtering through open canopies will add movement to a static formal scene. Silver birches, rowans and robinias like *Robinia pseudoacacia* 'Lace Lady' and the golden *R. pseudoacacia* 'Frisia' (which grow to 15m/50ft) allow dappled light to move across the garden space. For sheltered sites, the silver wattle (*Acacia dealbata*), at 10m (33ft), and varieties of *Acer japonicum* are elegant, lightly foliaged trees with well-shaped form.

multi-stemmed trees

A single tree may have its main stem cut back to the ground while young, to make an appropriate focus within a formal layout. This produces side-shoots that become a series of tree trunks, usually three. If, instead, three small saplings were planted together, they would compete for nutrition, with the winner growing tall while another may remain very stunted. Growing a multi-stemmed tree avoids this problem, each trunk usually being as strong as the others. Multi-stemmed trees have a lot of character and, used as single specimens, are much in demand for minimal gardens. Silver birches, in particular the white-stemmed *Betula utilis* var. *jacquemontii*, at 12m (39ft), are particularly effective used in this way but other small trees like *Acer negundo*, *Eucalyptus niphophila*, *Amelanchier lamarckii* and *Cercidiphyllum japonicum* also make attractive specimens.

   You need to decide whether to buy trees already grown in containers or wait until the autumn and plant them bare-rooted – either can be big or small. Container-grown trees will be more expensive due to the care lavished upon them in the nursery; though they will initially look more mature, tests suggest that the results will be the same within five years. Sizes commonly available are 'heavy standard', the trunks of which will have a girth of 12–15cm (5–6in), up to large, 'semi-mature' trees which will need guying, using pegged ropes and a sturdy rubber collar. Alternatively, you can grow them on yourself from a bare-rooted sapling, though you may risk losing them due to wind, frost or drought.

Four slim Swedish birches (Betula pendula 'Laciniata'), describe a square, reinforcing the geometry of a minimalist paved garden. The birches may be grown close together and, as they mature, the trunks will thicken and whiten, making a strong statement in front of the screen.

perennials & annuals

With so much angularity the modern formal garden needs some sparkle, particularly in summer. And those gardens that are elegantly minimal can benefit from the inclusion of just one plant that alters its appearance or sways in the breeze. Herbaceous plants fill this need and the best perennials can be integrated into a formal layout to soften it and give it a more contemporary feel. Bulbs and fast-growing annuals may also be used to ring the changes in a formal framework. (Quick effects with perennials and annuals, and the use of containers in the modern formal garden, are discussed in detail in Part 2, page 148.)

herbaceous perennials

Perennials are currently enjoying a revival of popularity. These plants have a reasonably long lifespan and will reappear every year, but they are less permanent and less rigid than shrubs, clipped or otherwise. On the whole, the perennials used in a modern formal context are not the flowers of the traditional herbaceous border but might include species grown for their unusual dark foliage or flower colour, such as dark-leaved heucheras and *Knautia macedonica*. How you use them will depend on the spirit of the garden and its scale, so their habit, size, texture and colours may be chosen with this in mind. Those that are architecturally dramatic are referred to earlier (see page 70).

foliage form

Neat effects can be achieved by using reliable perennials with clearly defined foliage as well as flowers. The satin-silver evergreen *Astelia nervosa* has sharply pointed but elegantly arching leaves; this plant grows to 60cm (2ft) but its silver leaves spread to a diameter of 1.5m (5ft). Though needing a warm site, it should not be fully exposed nor allowed to dry out completely. *Sisyrinchium striatum* also grows with finely ormed leaves in a two-dimensional fan pattern, emphasized by spikes of cream

82

far left *A metal sculpture rises from a mulch of lustrous blue glass beads surrounding a grid planting of the softly textured ornamental grass* **Stipa tenuissima.**

left *The erect grass* **Calamagrostis x acutiflora 'Stricta'** *aligned in planting troughs emphasizes the vertical metal trellis enclosing a rooftop. A multi-stemmed birch provides the focus.*

The herbaceous border still has a role in the modern formal garden. In these softly coloured twinned perennial borders planted by Arabella Lennox-Boyd, rich textures and strong forms hold together an exquisite scheme of copper and cream verbascums, cool yellow achilleas and dots of lilac-coloured alliums, with red-leaved heucheras and blue-leaved irises at their foot. The luminous colour harmony is maintained by white hesperis and wispy panicles of straw-coloured grasses that thread through the border.

flowers, 60cm (2ft) high, in early summer; the variegated form is particularly compact. *Iris pallida* 'Argentea Variegata', with lilac flowers in late spring, is similar but slightly larger. All the irises have interesting foliage, but placing the right plant in the right place is important because some irises like their tubers baked by the sun and others prefer to have light shade.

Other foliage types include the hazy background provided by feathery leaves like that of the culinary fennels and *Thalictrum lucidum*, with cream flowers in summer, growing up to 1.2m (4ft) high. The foliage of ferns or astilbes may be used to fringe taller shrubs with an attractive green lacy underskirt.

softening concrete austerity

The pink-washed courtyard garden designed by Beebe Yodell shows natural-looking, loose planting in a formal environment. It contains just a multi-stemmed olive tree with self-sown annual Californian poppies (*Eschscholzia californica*) growing in the random stone paving; crisply rosetted echeverias thrive in terracotta containers. The few plants used are drought-tolerant, often originating from arid landscapes.

colour

The formal garden is not the place for an uncontrolled 'riot of colour', nor for the multi-hued flamboyance of summer. It is basically green, with colour being used for a sympathetic background, harmonizing or contrasting with hard materials, or for powerful effects, to draw the eye. Colour can also be introduced to give a scheme sophistication, for example restricting it to monochrome or pastel shades, or to energize the garden, using flamboyant, saturated primaries. The white and green garden is chic and appropriately formal in its restraint. Silver foliage belongs here too, with white flowers like the gracefully rhythmical flower spikes of tall *Veronicastrum virginicum album* or white madonna lilies (*Lilium candidum*). Luminous greys, like those of artemisias, are important too; they suit gravelled schemes well, creating a Mediterranean look. This colouring is ideal with white-rendered concrete walls, slate floors or in association with steel or lime-washed timber.

Moody blues, such as that of the elegant *Campanula persicifolia* (1m/3ft tall), the shaded indigo of *Aconitum* 'Spark's Variety' (1.5m/5ft) or the inky blue *Salvia* x *sylvestris* 'Mainacht' (45cm/18in), have a cool effect which looks good with metals or slate; all are summer-flowering. With them plant steely eryngiums in galvanized containers. All of these would be superb if backed by yellow- or red-ochre rendered walls or in a more daring association with ultramarine-blue walls; they also look effective with flooring of terracotta tiles.

Plum-purples and brilliant magentas add richness and are dramatic against cream walls or blue-green slate paving. These colours are found in the midsummer-flowering *Iris* 'Black Swan' (80cm/2ft 8in tall), *Delphinium* Black Knight Group (1m/3ft 3in), *Geranium psilostemon* (75cm/2ft 6in) and the tender, deep maroon *Cosmos atrosanguineus* (60cm/2ft), flowering in late summer. If contrast is required, black floor tiling, blue-pink granite setts or dark timber would intensify the effect.

Hot, earthy colours are powerful, like those of late-summer *Helenium* 'Coppelia' (1.2m/4ft) and the midsummer-flowering *Hemerocallis* 'Morocco Red' and *Achillea millefolium* 'Paprika' (both 60cm/2ft). Plant these with bronze-leaved heucheras, to blend with brick and terracotta flooring or earth-coloured rendering. Dahlias will enrich any of these schemes towards the end of the season (see page 155).

85

Raised concrete beds run the length of a path in this superb garden designed by Christopher Bradley-Hole in which the symmetry of the planting ensures its formal character. On either side of the entrance, the thick brown trunks of old vines are silhouetted against white walls, while planting in the gravel-covered ground includes the strongly vertical forms of bearded irises, drumstick alliums and Nectaroscordum siculum, *with well-textured herbs like fennel and rosemary.*

texture

Texture has become a significant modern theme. Where the design is formal and the surfaces clearly geometric, it is the style of planting which will soften such severity. So hazy plants with tiny flowers, like gypsophila, or the wisp-fine foliage of fennel (*Foeniculum vulgare*), are in demand for their visual texture, performing as gently as a layer of filmy organza. Light is the key: as the sun moves around, the plants change character. Lit from the front, they are more noticeable but lit from behind the silhouette becomes a transparent screen through which other plants or features may be viewed. Texture can be tactile, too, like the furry leaves of *Stachys byzantina*. Irresistibly strokable plants like these soften the perception of the most clinical of layouts.

Ornamental grasses offer wonderful textural properties; they also have a long, late season and many can remain all winter to be sugared with frost. Of all garden plants, they are the most responsive to changing light effects, appealing to the senses of sight, sound and touch, ideal subjects for the understated perfection of modern gardens. Their flowers are often a myriad of tiny insubstantial culms, as with the 70cm (2ft 3in) high evergreen tufted hair grass (*Deschampsia cespitosa* 'Goldtau'), flowering early in summer. Others are more solidly structured, like the rounded fountain grasses (*Pennisetum*), especially the lovely *P. orientale* with a height and spread of 45cm (18in), whose late-summer flowers resemble furry foxtails. Some grasses are mopheaded, resembling tousled fine hair, such as the 60cm (2ft) high, summer-flowering feather grass (*Stipa tenuissima*). Others stand rigidly erect, like *Calamagrostis* x

acutiflora 'Stricta' which, on upright stems of 1.5m (5ft), provides delicate but firm contrast with floating midsummer grass flowers.

In the modern formal context ornamental grasses have proved to be ravishing animators of otherwise static scenes. Where clipped evergreen definition has a welcome simplicity, lines or grid patterns of grassy textures affect the scheme so that by late summer the picture is one of constant movement, with grass foliage responding to every air current while above hover fine hazy flowers, flickering with light. (Further ideas for using texture in formal gardens will be found in Part 2, page 135.)

annual effects

All gardens remind us of the passage of time and this continues in the new styles as well. Once the formal framework is established, the look of the garden alters seasonally, first with the spring freshness of bulbs, then through the summer high with flower colour. Autumn gives the garden a final warmth with its leaf colour and fruit. So during the year the whole character of the garden can change, making this a unique art form.

Bulbs like tulips lend themselves naturally to the geometry of the modern scene. With their sophisticated colours, they are a rich sight in spring and look magnificently formal when ranked in lines. They are also ideal for sparse planting effects, using small groups in selected spaces.

Lilies will admirably fit the bill for summer. There are many species and hybrids (see page 151), most of which prefer full sun and need good drainage; putting the bulbs on a mound of sharp sand is helpful. Alliums too will add formal character in summer, particularly the tall drumstick

Order is brought to a garden overflowing with mixed perennials and flowering shrubs by the strictly geometric box hedging which contains the planting.

opposite far left *Symmetrically planted borders have a soft formality, with grasses and artemisia offsetting flowering pernnials such as verbena, echinacea, sedum and asters. A central path is textured with houseleeks.*

opposite left *The deep blue of* Agapanthus inapertus *is intensified against rendered walls of midnight blue and cerulean blue, bringing seasonal drama to the garden.*

forms like *Allium giganteum*. As the season progresses, agapanthus will provide tall blue or white flowers emerging from green, strap-like foliage. All these carry themselves with a dignity appropriate to formal gardens. Plant bulbs at the right depth, usually two and a half times the bulb's height. If putting in large, expensive bulbs such as lilies, treat them against fungus and mice with a proprietary powder. Check soil drainage and plant them on coarse sand, if necessary, as in the case of lilies.

Some annuals with tall spikes have the same potential gravitas as the bulbs just referred to. Repeated upright forms suit an organized layout, so look for tall, slim flower spikes like those of foxgloves or *Moluccella laevis*. Colour can bring a formal plan alive as well and some annuals will do this almost instantly, such as antirrhinums or dahlias.

part 2 :interpretation

Modern formal gardens depend, as they always did, upon sound underlying organization set out by line. In the past line was used for practical reasons as well as ornamental ones, to make orderly functional divisions, for example separating culinary herbs from medicinal ones or terraces from lawns. Access paths always had a major role and lines were used to focus on vistas, while designs were mostly planned on geometric principles because right angles were satisfying. But the contemporary garden uses linear underpinning to explore the three-dimensional space of the garden as well as to lay out the flat ground plan. The whole garden, small or large, is divided, enclosed or pierced by lines that are the bones of the garden layout. Initially the lines are very strongly stated, by both hard landscape and soft planting, but as the garden matures they become partially concealed by plants and the formal layout becomes the subtle, almost unnoticed but essential order of the garden.

The architect Ron Herman took his inspiration for this elegantly planned garden from a chequerboard design of moss and stone seen in a Zen temple in Kyoto, Japan. The grid layout, outlined in bronze, defines the flat upper level of the terrace then gradually steps down to the lower levels, providing the cubic terracing seen here. Surface materials of smooth river pebbles contrast with rich green helxine (Soleirolia soleirolii). Below, the ground is covered by evergreen lilyturf (Ophiopogon japonicus 'Minor'), suiting the shady depths. Tall, slim bamboos rise from this lush groundcover, making further reference to Japan with their shadowy substance in front of a white wall.

In the old formality, planning was based on classical rules of scale and proportion, often including axial lines and perfect symmetry. Many gardens laid out in the European tradition were large and impressive, with long vistas, like those of Versailles in France or at Caserta, near Naples, in Italy. Others were small, enclosed, orderly collections of herbs and flowers. Whatever the scale, they were usually planned in a flat, decorative design to be viewed from above.

More recently, the strictly formal traditions of Mogul gardens were the inspiration for the huge Viceregal Garden laid out in New Delhi in the first half of the twentieth century by Sir Edwin Lutyens. The design, based on ceremonial symmetry, has intersecting grids made by water channels and regiments of clipped trees. Red sandstone edging around manicured lawns and rectangular flower beds reinforces the insistent geometry.

The evolution of the modern 'three-dimensional' garden began in the middle of the twentieth century, when significant developments in the world of the visual arts had permeated through to sculpture and architecture, eventually influencing garden design. New building materials like concrete were another part of the story. But, whatever the materials used, today's formal garden is often perceived primarily as an outdoor room, sharing the functions of daily life and reflecting the owner's style.

Modern formality uses line to enclose and define the private space in an architectural way, so the garden is felt to have walls, floor and ceiling. Far from being a framed, flat picture to be admired from the front, the visitor is encouraged to step into the 'room', to be involved in its care and to discover detail not seen from the house. Lines define spaces at all levels, whether on the ground, with steps and walls, or by overhead pergolas. All areas are made accessible by being organized on a linear basis, leading one to explore the site and creating a shift of emphasis towards participation and simplicity in place of admiration and ornament.

scale

Today's gardens range from mere balconies or tiny courtyards to acres of land immersed in the countryside. But since gardens are not natural places, a design based on formality can be just as relevant in large country gardens as in small, contained spaces. Modern formality means planning boldly and reaching out to the landscape, while also considering

lines & layout

Two long, slim rills of water on either side of a central pergola walk define the linear design of this garden. Parallel lines of pleached limes reinforce the symmetry and lead into the depths of the garden.

the architectural geometry of the house. The large scale calls for subtle order, for example planning a wide vista to a far focus, emphatically bordered by clipped hedging or parallel pergolas. Lines of lesser importance may cross the central path, dividing the area into smaller units and leading away to enclosures on either side.

Organized formality near the building, like a terrace, sets off a house well and provides a comfortable space that is in scale with the building. In contemporary terms this means an uncluttered area closely associated with the garden, without the separation of a balustrade. All planting should relate to the geometry of the house, using immaculate, well-structured material (see the suggestions for clippable plants, page 64), getting more relaxed as the garden leads away to the rural view.

But large spaces are less common today and it is the smaller end of the scale that is the major focus of modern garden design. The twentieth century saw gardening become accessible for all, the private plot being viewed as an extension to the house. In his concrete homes of the 1930s, the architect Le Corbusier provided open courtyards and roof gardens that related geometrically to the house and were in scale with indoor rooms. He stressed the essential simplicity of such functional spaces, saying that areas must be set aside for people and furniture, leaving space for planting and none for unnecessary decoration. The scale of the smaller garden made these recreational spaces workable and manageable, allowing people to enjoy plants and share meals in seclusion.

Whatever its dimensions, as long as the garden plan has a formal foundation, in scale with the building and people, the planting should be chosen to enhance the layout. Spacious gardens may hold tall specimens, like the wide, large-leaved Indian bean tree (*Catalpa bignonioides*), ultimately 9m by 6m (30ft by 20ft), or the lovely *Cornus kousa* var. *chinensis*, 7m (22ft) high. But small-scale areas should not be planted on a miniature Lilliputian scale because such fussiness is never comfortable – a garden should relate to people, rather than to its size.

The intimate urban garden of today tends to be inward-looking, but people should still feel able to walk through or pause to rest without feeling cramped. Boundaries will feel less confining if they are made to 'vanish', concealed by evergreen wall shrubs like pyracantha, ceanothus and escallonia, making the area appear larger. And actual scale may be distorted by playing with trick perspectives, to exaggerate depth. Another way to confuse the reality of scale is with the use of mirrors to reflect lines, forms and areas of the garden, creating a formal symmetry. The frame of the mirror must be concealed by foliage or tucked within an 'arch' to make the illusion effective. The garden is thus visually extended through 'openings' that are not there.

Plants too can be used to deceive. Despite a garden being small, dramatic impact is created with an oversized plant like giant fennel (*Ferula communis*) with its solitary stem of branched yellow umbels up to 2.5m (8ft) tall; it must have good drainage, and be grown in full sun. As plants may be oversized, so too can containers; placed away from the house, they will draw the eye. Consider choosing a huge Ali Baba clay pot as a striking focal sculpture; these are expensive, so be sure they are frostproof for cold areas. Where space is at a premium, raised plant troughs, to 40cm (16in) high, can be built in, to fit with the geometric ground plan, making the fitted garden as efficient as the fitted kitchen.

lines

In every garden, whether inadvertently or by design, the underlying order is set by line. It divides and rules, creating units, marking out levels, directing the eye and setting objectives. And it powerfully affects the spirit of a garden, depending on whether it is strong, subtle or fluid. Line is emphatic in the modern garden and has a dual role: it meets mundane needs practically and sets the creative impact of the scene.

Formality usually means that lines will be at right angles or in parallel and everything in the garden follows this formula, from hard landscaping to plants. This no longer necessarily implies symmetry. Once there would have been a central axis, down which a path or *allée* could be seen to its end, dividing the garden into two. This serious symmetry is too heavy for the modern garden, so lines usefully link or separate areas as paths, walls, steps, hedges or edges. Because they are so visible, they also lead the eye around the space, emphasizing the aesthetics of the design.

Taking the lines of a garden layout from those of the house is a useful way of setting out the design and tying in house and garden. Internal subdivisions or doors, verandahs, windows and balconies will all indicate proportions that can provide the foundation for a formal design. Ground

Starkly effective in a winter garden, this strongly geometric design has clipped crab apples (Malus 'Adams') growing through raised timber plinths, laid in a grid. Cylindrical planters create repeated verticals.

lines that relate to the property are made with walls, fences, screens, paving layout, planting beds and hedges. Overhead lines foster the link, with timber or steel beams and pergolas carrying climbers. Line may be continuous – like a length of retaining wall in a two-level garden – or it may be suggested by a visual link across a plant mass or an empty space.

Line can also resolve problems. For example, gardens allotted to a house rarely have accurately parallel boundaries and some plots are more of a narrow strip, a triangle or a bent dog-leg in shape. 'Imperfections' such as these can be resolved by a formal layout that ignores boundaries, so that the design relates geometrically to the house and awkward left-over areas are concealed by evergreens.

paths

Paths draw the lines of the garden but, if they are only a functional straight line between two points, can spoil its charm. In modern gardens, paths become an invitation, a means of exploring and discovering the unexpected. Even small gardens benefit if all is not revealed at first glance. There must be some magic, such as turning a path sharply out of sight around a hedge or fence, enticing us to investigate what lies unseen.

Main paths are normally about 1m (3ft 3in) wide but I prefer them to be wider, 1.2m (4ft) or more, to be able to walk alongside a companion. I also like the clarity of width, particularly when edging flat grass. And wide paths allow unrestrained foliage to blur the edges along their length, softening the formality. At the other extreme, there is a strong case for squeezing extremely narrow paths between hedges, intimately enclosing a single person and suggesting a dramatic opening beyond.

Lines that make routes can affect progress. In all gardens, parts of the site are less interesting than others, so we may dally to regard beauty, in the form of a plant or a view, or pass on quickly where there is less to interest us. Curved lines powerfully control our pace and, as part of the circumference of a circle, they suit modern formal gardens. The smaller the circle, the tighter the curve, which fosters speedy progress to exciting areas, whereas sweeping curves slow the journey, so we may contemplate.

Once the formal plan is established, lines can be reinforced with plants, like parallels of formally clipped hedging, as described in Part 1 (see page 64), to emphasize a major path or sight line. In a smaller site dwarf hedging is as effective: parallel planting of lavender or santolina

top *Flattened box edging is boldly clipped into diagonal lines that narrow almost to a point, framing a wedge-shaped pool.*

above *The 'Physics Garden', designed by Charles Jencks, is a unique interpretation of a kitchen garden in which he explores the senses. Certain concepts recur throughout, like designing with fractals, which contributes to the linear quality of the planting, while the spiralling sculptures translate the theory of the structure of DNA.*

on diagonal lines

Parallel lines of low box hedging, 45cm (18in) high, create a dynamic effect in this small garden space. Planting in diagonals increases the area available for people to use and a taller box hedge, 1.5m (5ft) high, also screens the shed at the back. Square concrete paving is laid at 45 degrees with the house to reinforce the linear design and create the sense of a spacious inner courtyard for sitting. Here a specimen *Robinia pseudoacacia* 'Bessoniana' is the focus over an evergreen groundcover of *Walsteinia ternata*, while the small *Prunus mumi* 'Omoi-no-mama' delights by the house in spring from a ground cover of *Asplenium scolopendrium* Undulatum Group. Wall shrubs like *Chaenomeles speciosa* 'Nivalis', *Garrya elliptica* 'James Roof', *Clematis armandii* 'Snowdrift' and, facing south, *Itea ilicifolia*, adorn the rendered walls. At the north end, triangular spaces are filled with clipped *Osmanthus delavayi* to provide formal structure and fragrance in spring. Long planting beds are filled with herbaceous perennials for seasonal effect and three 'tanks' are planted with spring bulbs or summer-flowering lilies.

This part of the garden previously shown in winter (page 93) turns a change of level into a design asset, resolved by simple geometry. Steps, outlined with granite setts, merge into square planting beds holding clipped Malus 'Adams' with lime-washed trunks.

hedges would reinforce a formal layout and help to clarify routes as well as separate plants from paving. This may be accented by rows of clipped lollipop bay trees or standard fuchsias at regular intervals. A regiment of standard weeping *Cotoneaster salicifolius* 'Pendulus' would be stylish, having semi-evergreen trailing branches that are wreathed in flowers or red berries; they grow ultimately to 3m (10ft) high. The horizontally branching cherry *Prunus* 'Shogetsu' can make a cloistered tunnel, with low vaults created by the branches which are laden with sprays of white flowers in spring and with colourful autumn foliage. Barely reaching 5m (15ft), it has a width of 9m (30ft). Timber pergolas are another means of emphasizing a straight route, adding three-dimensional overhead lines.

Not every compact courtyard will have paths but the lines of the design can still underlie appearance, for example in the way paving is laid in relation to the house. Judiciously placed contained plants are a good way of suggesting the garden's linear structure: the eye follows a visual 'line' in moving from one to another. Rows of identical planters set out like the contained orange trees in Italian Renaissance gardens though on a smaller scale (see opposite), will emphasize line all year round if planted with domes of clipped box. The plants could be changed for seasonal effect, but resist introducing too much variety. Formality is best served by repeat plantings, like potted lavenders in full sun or dramatic cordylines in larger containers. For shade, ferns like *Polystichum setiferum* or grasses like *Hakonechloa macra* 'Aureola' are suited to rhythmical order.

Planning on diagonal lines creates less tranquil, more dynamic gardens. There is an urgency that takes the eye across the garden, ricocheting from feature to feature. Not traditionally formal, diagonal organization introduces a different contemporary order and has positive uses. Diagonals make small gardens seem larger and often make better use of an area, so more can be fitted in. Used in narrow gardens, they effectively increase apparent width and draw the visitor into the space.

grids

Another approach uses line in a very different way, creating a passive garden style with an overall effect, without path or focus. Mathematical order is dominant in today's formal gardens, and the simplicity of a grid appeals, provided it is in scale with the site. In large gardens, the grid is a simple geometric composition that covers a square space with pattern.

top **Planted on a strict grid, inert balls of small 'pincushion' cacti (Echinocactus grusonii) are dramatic in this square parterre-like enclosure, which is a detail of a garden designed by Martha Schwartz.**

above **The spare planting of a formal orchard is simply reinforced by mowing the grass to create a square grid layout. The trees are on the intersections of the closely mown paths, while wildflowers grow in longer grass.**

Underpinned with identical plants on each intersection, the lines of a grid hold a space together. Unlike the power of a central line or symmetry, grid lines lead nowhere, and no line is more important than any other, making a design that is tranquillity itself.

In the larger formal garden a grid may be laid out very simply using trees, rather like an orchard, to create a rhythmical order that is made three-dimensional by the covering canopy layer. Looking through the grid of columnar tree trunks beneath the canopy is a pleasurable experience.

Shafts of light create flickering movement on the ground and seasonal changes mark the passage of time. The American landscaper Dan Kiley used grids widely in many of his superb modern schemes, often choosing trees such as the fine-leaved honey locust (*Gleditsia triacanthos*), 15m (50ft) tall, or wide-spreading hawthorns like *Crataegus persimilis* 'Prunifolia', growing to 8m (27ft). Mophead acacias (*Robinia pseudoacacia* 'Umbraculifera') suit smaller sites, with a height and spread of 6m (20ft). They have no canopy but emerge effectively from a flat grassed area

open to the sky. Another layer, between ground and canopy, may be added if each tree is planted centrally in a plinth of clipped box, about 60cm (2ft) high (see the photograph on page 69). Geometric groves like these are also suitable for paved areas, where the intersecting grid provides a natural site for shaded corner seats with a built-in table.

In small gardens square paving set out in a simple grid is anonymous, never dominating the space, but a chequerboard scheme gives style to compact modern plots. Low clipped cubes of box may be maintained about 45cm (18in) high or flat areas of creeping thyme interspersed with square flagstones of the same dimensions, say 45–60cm (18in–2ft). Carpeting thymes may be walked upon but, if this is not a requirement, the squares may be attractive filled with hardy houseleeks (*Sempervivum tectorum*) for cold districts or tender *Echeveria elegans* for warmer ones. All three need full sun and gritty, well-drained soil. Trailing small-leaved ivies are another alternative, clipped into low squares at ground level.

There has been a revival of interest in mazes in modern gardens and they are entirely a matter of line, whether rectangular, spiral, concentric or three-dimensional. They add an intangible atmosphere rather than just pattern but this is discussed further in the next chapter (see page 122).

geometric spaces

The past ideal of the picturesque scene was a series of flat planes, to be admired from a viewpoint. Where the grand symmetrical gardens, based on a central axis, divided an area equally, the focus was on the main dividing path, itself crossed by less significant parallel routes. The reduced areas and the lines separating them made surface patterns which became more important than the overall garden space. And the paisley swirls and fleur-de-lys of box-edged parterres were like icing on a cake, decorative and two-dimensional. Their symmetrical patterns were never intended to be more than an embroidery effect, richly coloured and textured but flat.

As garden sites became smaller, the fashion for gardens with an open central lawn, framed by planted borders, emulated the past and became the accepted norm. Sometimes there were island beds cut out of the flat carpeting turf, decoratively reminiscent of parterres. But the real space of the garden was not fully exploited and it was not inviting.

Pattern making is no longer the aim and today's garden layout is both more exciting and more involving. It creates a three-dimensional, formally

opposite A spare, geometric approach to the design of a pool without ornament reveals the tranquillity of still water, seen here in early morning light.

Three sides of a lawn are outlined by a narrow water channel, in a design by the author. The immaculate paving is precision-cut Cumbrian green slate, while red salvias provide planting detail in a damp pebble-covered bed.

The tapering triangular garden is an awkward shape to plant but this scheme resolves the difficulty by a totally linear plan. Clipped balls of grey Santolina chamaecyparissus make parallel lines that lead into the distance on either side of the path. Clipped green Santolina rosmarinifolia continues the lines but also wittily cuts across them to create an apex that is the focus of the garden.

defined space planned on geometric principles where people can look up, down and all around; they appreciate being in garden spaces that are 'rooms without ceilings'. Taking a lead from modern architecture, try to balance the mass of features and plant material by spacious voids, the irreplaceable ingredient of contemporary gardens.

planning the layout

A blank sheet of paper, like the empty car park, fosters indecision. So help yourself by acknowledging that it is not necessary to fill every corner with plants because empty areas will balance the energy of the growing mass. For the practical designer, first decisions are similar to those inside the house – a need to screen service areas. The space left over can then be divided between recreation and plants; only the user will know which is more important. If the two areas are the same size, the garden will be bland and uninteresting, but by making one larger than the other, the layout immediately becomes less predictable and more exciting.

Contemplate a contrast between a large, restful space with a smaller, densely packed one. Or make the more spacious part very detailed, adjacent to a small, secluded sitting area. Decide whether to mark the division by a change of surface material or to enclose one of the spaces, either for privacy or wind protection. Natural light helps to define forms and spaces – the dark depths will appear limitless in contrast to the open, light-filled areas which are more inviting. For a geometric layout, define

100

top *A concrete edging to square pavers allows a waved outline to one side of the pool.*

above *Low terracing follows the natural contours of the land, supported by walls of woven willow that create a series of flat beds.*

Dramatically sharp points can present problems, but here gravel flows easily around the curved bed planted with Verbena bonariensis.

flowing curves

A small rear garden is planned with curvaceous spaces laid with resin-bonded buff-coloured gravel. Steps extend from one side of the garden to the other, with narrow treads in the centre that widen in an organic sweep, vanishing into the plants on either side. Edged with concrete setts, they lead down from the sitting area beside the house into the open space ending in a raised pool. The terrace, only 25cm (10in) above the rest of the garden, is high enough to see the surface of the water, itself 40cm (16in) high.

The slow-growing, hardy evergreen snow gum (*Eucalyptus pauciflora* subsp. *niphophila*), is a dramatic focus, with leathery grey-turquoise leaves and a smooth white trunk. It can be pruned to within three buds of the base in early spring to make a bush with juvenile rounded leaves.

The still, jaggedly shaped pool is a stark contrast, its sharp point hidden behind plants. A mahogany-stained timber bench seat follows the line of the pool at the same height, gradually tapering as it vanishes into the planting. The surrounding beds are planted with pampas grasses.

Sinuous, organically curved lines of low clipped box flow out in rhythmically repeated waves, edging a lawn with great distinction in this garden designed by Daniël Ost.

and enclose space with right-angled structures, using timber, brick, concrete or glass walls and screens, or, more gently, with hedges. Once special areas have been planned, people can be drawn into them through entrances which may be widely inviting or narrowly seductive.

In the larger garden, uninterrupted lawns can be just as enticing as spaces of more intimate proportions and such simplicity is well within the aim of modern formality. An open space is tranquil whether rectangular or smoothly circular. Nothing need interrupt it except, perhaps, a specimen tree; I would suggest this is not planted centrally but closer to the boundary, where the canopy will link it to another part of the garden.

In smaller modern plots, gravel or paving often stand in for lawns. Such hard surfacing may look too harsh in cold or wet countries, so allow carpet plants like *Thymus serpyllum* or *Pratia pedunculata* to roam and soften the gravel effect. For a softening association with paving slabs, clipped dwarf hedging, such as silvery *Santolina chamaecyparissus* or green *S. rosmarinifolia*, would maintain the formality but could also cramp the sense of space. So consider allowing a stretch of grass, gravel or paving to run right up to the boundary. Where they meet, the fence or wall may be screened with evergreen ivy, 'losing' the garden's limitations and greening its vertical dimension.

Tall structures can enclose smaller spaces and hide views so that not everything is seen at a glance. Consider blocking out some areas with fences or formally clipped hedges like yew or evergreen *Osmanthus* x *burkwoodii*, with its scented white flowers and dense foliage. Other areas may be partially revealed by transparent screening, described in Part 1 (see page 37), or enclosed seasonally by tall ornamental grasses like *Miscanthus floridulus*, to make a summer place of secluded intimacy.

The three-dimensional 'volume' of the garden can be integrated overhead by tree canopies or with timber or metal beams, supported by posts or attached to the house wall. Similar to pergolas, these structures tie in with the garden layout as skeletal sculpture, defining a right-angled, three-dimensional expanse, graphically etched against the sky. Beams may be left unclothed but if you want a climber, avoid the rustic look of honeysuckle-covered romanticism and choose instead bold foliage like that of the giant-leaved Japanese glory vine (*Vitis coignetiae*).

organic spaces

Pure geometry is not the only influence that gave rise to the modern garden. There were some periods in English garden history when it was replaced by 'natural order', as in the eighteenth-century Arcadian landscapes of Capability Brown and Humphrey Repton. But a totally fresh inspiration came from Japan at the end of the nineteenth century. Japanese woodblock prints circulating in Europe, often as wrappings for tea, revealed different artistic values and a new way to create a highly organized space, based on the fluid asymmetries found in nature. The influence of Japanese gardens was also invigorating, freeing garden design from geometric constraints and emphasizing the spirit of the site.

The Zen gardens of the classical era reveal a sensitive observation of nature and an eloquence that referred to the organically formed landscape (see The Japanese Effect, page 147). They were made and maintained with meticulous attention to detail but great restraint. The lie of the land, with its curves and undulations, provides the inspiration. Little is straight in nature and lines that could never be drawn by a pair of compasses make gentle spaces, usually without right angles or symmetry. Wavy lines that are entirely decorative have no power, tension or contrast between softness and strength, whereas 'organic' lines, implyingy uneven growth, may be stretched or taut, sweeping or tight, simple or fragmented. These are not easy to draw on a plan, so try to develop them from natural forms like flintstone or the grain of wood, with rocks or plants interrupting their flow. Avoid edging areas and paths – there are no tidy edges to a stream or woodland – but savour the natural spread of ground-hugging plants or gravels that form amorphous curves.

This alternative approach to highly ordered garden design is far less space-dividing than using pure geometry. It can be likened to snapshot views as caught by the camera, revealing that large, empty areas can dominate a scene and yet beautifully balance the small details within it. Always show restraint – Zen traditions of asymmetry grew from nature but the art of creating a very special formal order lies in the simple harmony and balance imposed by man.

top ***Nature, not geometry, is the inspiration for this 'Japanese' landscape. Sharply emerging rocks, jutting out from the sea of raked gravel, have a dynamic and tense relationship, but a single recumbent rock holds a small pool of dew in this atmospheric garden.***

above ***In a design by Cleve West, this garden path, made of impeccably laid granite setts, swings around the curved outline of the lawn, drawing the visitor into the light beyond.***

The basic requirements of the contemporary formal garden are essentially the same as those of the past. Modern geometrically planned schemes still draw on the European tradition of straight-line vistas leading to a delightful focus: a temple, statue or urn. Planned routes and views are used much as they were in the past, albeit on a different scale; areas of rest will always be required; bosky groves need the counterbalance of open spaces. Planting may still be decorative, impressive or represent collections; water will take the form of fountains, waterfalls, fish ponds and terrace pools. This remarkable heritage has not been rejected but, as will be shown, simply reset in a different mode, adjusted to the new century.

George Carter designed this contemporary garden that harks back to other traditions, playing with Gothic and oriental imagery through white-painted timber.

changed expectations

Though the functions of today's gardens are much as they always have been, our lives are conducted on more rational principles and we live on a smaller scale. Contemporary gardens are generally planned for domestic living and will be maintained by the owner. They tend to be smaller, cost less to create and to run but they are highly personal. Individuality matters more than status today and, consequently, the expectations of contemporary garden owners are very different from those of estate owners of the past. Since we care for our gardens ourselves, fussy detail is to be avoided; flounces and finials belong to history. So while there may still be a need for a terrace to sit on, a stone balustrade would sit too pompously for modern thinking. The provision of an easily managed, three-dimensional, comfortable and inviting space is far more important than ornamentation.

Contemporary town gardens in particular tend to be simply planned, often with built-in furniture of concrete, brick or timber. Boundaries and spatial divisions are frequently geometric, tightly linked with the house, and the materials used may be stone, decking or concrete. Planting beds may be raised for access and the design is plain and unfussy, often depending on allowing the planting to soften the whole area.

scale

In the past little existed between huge estates planned on grand lines and basic cottage gardens that fed the family. But now the gap is increasingly filled with garden sizes varying from balconies and town courtyards, through typical suburban plots to country gardens of several acres.

Small is not an entirely new concept, however, because in the past large gardens were often divided into inward-looking enclosures or courts, with a central well or fountain. Today's secluded small gardens are treated as open-air rooms, geared to efficient outdoor living. Despite the diminished size of the average garden, our expectations have increased so that practical needs have to be served as well as relaxation offered. There are wonderful country gardens, flourishing suburban strips, serviceable small courtyards and even tiny balconies planned to entertain friends, all of which are being designed on a human, accessible scale. A lot has to be fitted in, requiring designs that are both simplified and condensed.

traditionally innovative

left *An obelisk that could have graced an eighteenth-century formal garden is the main focus for a small, symmetrical urban courtyard. It is central to a raised water tank, reminiscent of classical Portuguese gardens, from which water falls into a ground-level pool below. A grid pattern defines the slate paving.*

opposite *Dan Pearson designed this rooftop with a deck for people and steel-drum planters for multi-stemmed birches. The rest of the space holds mounds of plants that emerge from flat groundcover.*

Smaller spaces have also led to the vertical planting of climbers and wall shrubs that use and cover every upright surface and boundary. Beams can replace the old pergolas, now fixed to the walls to carry these climbers out into the space of the garden, without the need for uprights.

utility, cost and management

The large gardens of the past were created as extensions of a wealthy lifestyle. They had to impress, whereas today the emphasis is on a pleasing ambience. For all who love gardens the expectation is that they fulfil dreams as well as bringing living outdoors in the summer. But the cost must be realistic. And while in the past gardens often depended on the employment of gardeners, in the interest of economy most of us now do the work ourselves, and we find the formal layout of the modern garden easy to control.

The chosen materials can lead the style. For example, if you like cream limestone paving, you are likely to go for a minimalist approach where everything will be cool and pale, with accompanying materials similarly immaculate: white rendered walls, for example, would be freshly painted at the start of the season when the flagstones are pressure cleaned. Features of polished steel or sand-blasted opaque glass panelling are easily maintained and a quick wipe-over will restore the pristine standard of appropriate furniture. Plant ingredients should be similarly easy to look after, the majority of them being well-formed evergreens like magnolias or shapely fan palms.

On the other hand, the choice of decking as a floor surface would indicate that you prefer a slightly warmer, more relaxed feel, perhaps with other natural materials and terracotta-washed rendered walls. You may accept a certain degree of dishevelment in order that maintenance does not become onerous. So, for example, leaf fall is not seen as a disaster, slatted timber furniture can be covered with cushions and a canvas awning may be used to diffuse the light of the sky. Soft plants might include elegantly branching acers or responsive bamboos.

management It was in the first half of the twentieth century that artists of the Bauhaus aesthetic decreed that modern homes should be easy to manage – and this included the gardens that went with them. Gardens were designed to take account of this, making functional spaces that served the owner's needs, rather than imitating the luxury of past times. Though still in essence a 'pleasure garden', the space must work for us practically.

Formality is the perfect starting point and modernism, with its insistence upon coherent simplicity, is the ideal principle on which to plan a manageable garden. We expect there to be room for essentials, like oil tanks, compost heaps and storage sheds, while maintaining a precious outdoor place of charm and beauty which is a pleasure to sit in. The small 'fitted garden' fulfils a practical need, with built-in furniture that doubles as raised planters and small pools fountain-fed from a spout in the wall. Walls of glass bricks, coloured rendered concrete, closely set

timber posts or panels of trellis or woven willow all serve to screen utilities and be attractive in their own right.

Well-planned garden management is essential to retain the cool refinement of modern formality. Good storage facilities make it a simple matter to put garden tools and packable chairs away; they are easily concealed if geometrically organized spaces include a line of screening. Formality also means fewer details and clear spaces, so less detritus will tend to accumulate. Careful choice of materials can help enormously.

left *Marble paving provides a bridge over a lily pool to the loggia beyond. This allusion to classical Italian garden style is emphasized by the traditional colouring of the terracotta-washed wall, in front of which are modern versions of classical columns.*

opposite *The classically inspired and proportioned but modern vine-clad arbour offers a sheltered place for secluded, alfresco dining overlooking mixed Mediterranean planting.*

Traditionally, algae-covered stone and moss-covered brick pavers were thought romantic, as long as someone else cleaned them. Now, most well-jointed, smooth, hard surfaces are easy to sweep or hose down, which is a boon in a dry, dusty summer. But if your hard floors are pale limestone flags, for example, there are companies that will undertake once- or twice-yearly pressure cleaning. Gravel is tidy for most of the year, but when covered by fallen leaves in autumn it requires painstaking removal by hand of the larger leaves, followed by raking. Wooden decks always have spaces beneath them so they are easily brushed clean (though food remnants should not be brushed down because they will attract rodents).

Glossy or painted surfaces like wood and metal furniture can be wiped or washed down quickly, but you should expect to have to repaint them every few years because the paint may peel off in extreme weather conditions. On the other hand, subtle stains will gradually fade into the body of the material so there should be no need for touching up. Any surface that needs repainting – like rendered walls or painted trellis – should be kept clear of the type of plant that adheres by tendrils, such as vigorous ivies, or that tangle into other plants, like the vigorous climbing *Clematis montana*.

time Available time must be considered and many gardeners expect to manage their gardens over the weekend. So the formally modern garden, planted with compact evergreen shrubs and some architectural perennials, prettied up with spring bulbs and summer annuals, is a formula that does not get out of control very quickly. Clipped box hedging also helps to maintain a neat garden, even after a lengthy period of holiday neglect.

privacy

Many people describe their garden as a safe haven – somewhere to cut them off from the intrusions of daily life, where they may lift the drawbridge and be tranquil. With the mobile phone left indoors, the garden becomes a treasured island. This is one of the most important expectations of contemporary life and the modern formal garden, with its order and quiet simplicity, is the place to achieve it. Walls conceal what lies inside, unless they are transparent, and provide secluded enclosures. Evergreens, clipped like solid masonry, help to baffle sound, spacious seating relaxes the spirit and the use of water invites contemplation. Above all, a garden that is as orderly and pleasingly simple as those built in a formal contemporary manner makes few demands. Most of us like to have uninterrupted peace on returning home.

appealing to the senses

We expect more from our gardens than that they are simply restorative and that they work satisfactorily. It is the element of personal indulgence that separates the modern garden from those of the past. Since early times, gardens have fulfilled the need for sheer pleasure and the art of the garden appeals inherently to the senses – so, in the first place, its appearance must please. And while some contemporary gardens may be tranquil, others are full of vitality, creating the unpredictable and establishing a mood as much by means of colour, fragrance and other sensory qualities as by their extravagance of line or their exploration of innovative materials.

Every material used in the garden will have a colour, whether it is the natural self-colouring of timber or stone or applied colour on a wall or a seat. Colours affect mood but, because moods change, the choice of colours must please at all times. Red and orange, for example, may be exciting in winter, but hard to take in the heat of summer. So earth reds, those ochre shades like rust or terracotta, are a softer solution. Yellow is a reminder of sunlight on grey days but, again, the ochres are a subtle way of enjoying this hue, while pale lemons and almost neutral straw colours are very pleasant in the garden context. Blues offer a range of cool, sophisticated shades and tones and strong mid-blue is popular in today's gardens, especially for furniture and pergolas, possibly because

left *The wide grass path, with stilt hedges on either side, draws the visitor to a circular summer pavilion in this garden designed by David Hicks. True to modern formality, all features are simple and unadorned, including the wide, shallow steps lined with low clipped box hedging.*

opposite *A detail of the George Carter garden seen on page 69 shows a narrow, still 'canal' leading to a dark niche containing a mask sculpture. The plan is severely linear but silver-grey artemisias and Stachys byzantina, with a canopy of London plane foliage, have a gentling effect, punctuated by the reflected gleam of Georgina Miller's polished aluminium 'floating boulder'.*

of its association with Moorish architecture. Artificial greens are difficult to use in gardens because of the range of verdant foliage hues, but if darkened to 'bottle' green, the depth of this colour sets off plants well.

Any very strong colour may 'take over' the garden so consider softer neutrals like greys, rust-browns, pinky-beiges and creamy-ochres. Black and white are appropriate in minimal gardens and look dramatic in a contemporary space using green slate and stainless steel. But they need not be stark absolutes: even a risky chocolate shade would be classy with old red sandstone flags and faded pink-washed rendered walls.

Flower colour is special and in the modern garden summer extremes can be vibrant. Consider scarlet *Crocosmia* 'Lucifer' with inky *Iris* 'Sable Night' or a clash of wine-red *Iris* 'Langport Claret'. These erect, mid-height plants have sword-like foliage that suits a regimented formality. If a sophisticated pallor is wanted, think about ranks of *Tulipa* 'White Triumphator' to enhance a group that changes as summer progresses, to be replaced by a repeat pattern of fanning *Sisyrinchium striatum* with cream flower spikes in early summer, followed by stiffly vertical *Kniphofia* 'Green Jade' or taller, pinkish *Veronicastrum virginicum* for late summer.

Fragrance appeals on another level without adding any visual detail to the simple lines of the modern formal garden. Winter scents like those of compact evergreen *Sarcococca humilis*, a useful shade plant, are lovely on a mild day. Many magnificent magnolias are richly fragrant in spring and when summer comes there are so many flowers, from lavenders to lilies, that continue to fill a courtyard with scents. Choose those that fulfil the formal requirements of the site as well and the expectations for a fragrant modern garden will be satisfied.

reinterpreted elements

We never completely shake off the legacies of the recent past; indeed, gradual evolution is seen as a good way forward. Conservatism and reproduction play no part here – we are referring to reinterpreting the past with energy and imagination. The respected twentieth-century British garden designer Russell Page was a master of such designing, as his gardens around the world testify. And today new voices have developed that refer back, discarding the irrelevant, adding fresh new ideas and giving a contemporary twist to traditional ingredients that brings them right up to date.

Modern formality is less predictable than before: the lines of organization are surprising, frequently asymmetrical and may flout convention; wit is often evident and things may not be quite as they appear. Pergolas, arbours, stretches of grass, pools, fountains and enclosures are still sought today but there are new twists on these traditional features as well as eclectic references to the past. Living linear divisions provide small garden rooms, while the limitless expansion of three-dimensional topiary is all part of the contemporary formal garden. Other cultures have been cheerfully plundered, like the narrow water channels of Mogul gardens, providing thin rills, the pleached lime trees of France outlining geometric space and the Japanese appreciation of nature expressed with exquisite aesthetic economy.

axes and vistas

The concept of *allées* and avenues implies symmetry, suggesting the essential plan of the garden. If such symmetry appeals to you, bear in

mind that it will dominate everything, allowing the eye no alternative place to settle but the central line. So you will need to tailor all other requirements and features to fit your particular space.

Entering a formal garden space to face a direct path invites exploration along it. Traditionally the axis would have been reinforced on either side with well-spaced hedges flanked by monuments of clipped yews. In the modern courtyard there may be no room for tall stilt hedges but a bold adaptation of this idea can achieve the same dramatic result. For example, a centrally placed wide strip of coursed granite setts can mark out a direct 'path' among squares of paving. To either side of the granite strip, long straight runs of pygmy bamboo, like *Pleioblastus pygmaeus* var. *disticus*, will emphasize the symmetry while the rampant root run of the bamboo is restrained by the paving. On both sides of the courtyard, timber posts and wires running parallel with the path could carry trained triple lines of wisteria, adding flowers in early summer. At the far end the lines of small grassy bamboo may open out to form a spacious rectangle, outlined by a taller bamboo, to provide an enclosure for seating and dining. The far boundary, now a wall of bamboo, is where the eye will rest and this would be a perfect site for a simple erect timber sculpture among the canes. Light the seating area well (see page 58) but use soft downlighting along the bamboo, just enough for safety.

A radically different approach would be to celebrate the *space* of a garden totally enclosed by glass brick walls with timber deck flooring – a few container-grown plants and some furniture would be the only detail. With no central focal feature, the space at the far end becomes the focus and simply walking into the space is enough.

In some outward-looking gardens, vistas in the form of 'borrowed' distant features, like a church spire, can be the set piece. In such a case, make it absolutely clear that this is the focus and be sure that all planting or features on either side are identical. Flatter the view by a low frame of evergreen *Choisya* 'Aztec Pearl' below, with perhaps matching taller hedges of beech or clipped topiary to frame the sides.

One very small garden that I designed is wider than it is deep, but it was still planned with geometric symmetry, that appears to add depth (see plan on page 138). Slim rectangular limestone paving runs parallel with the house, petering out randomly into planted areas. On either side, twinned 'buttresses' of clipped *Osmanthus delavayi* divide the walls

top *Beech hedging in a garden designed by Erik Dhont creates magical spaces and enclosures.*

above *A modern turf maze implies primitive mystical associations, planned in a design inspired by very early labyrinthine rock engravings.*

interrupted maze

This square courtyard garden, with its circular design, is planned to be seen from above. The concentric rings of clipped box are left incomplete, creating a restless feeling of continual movement. This modern adaptation of a maze introduces confusion, so that the visitor may choose the route to the central focus. But the paving – a strong statement of rectangular cut and randomly sized York stone, laid in a coursed pattern – and the rectangular, pergola-enclosed entrance stabilize the design.

The garden pivots around a multi-stemmed *Betula papyrifera*, its focal point. Shrubs like clematis, *Chaenomeles speciosa* and *Euonymus fortunei* 'Silver Queen' clothe the walls and a run of bamboo (*Pleioblastus viridistriatus*) is contained by the paving. Clipped box provides a rotating framework, with small topiary as markers or stopping points. Less structured herbaceous planting follows the movement. Plants like *Crocosmia* 'Lucifer', *Sisyrinchium striatum* and *Liriope muscari* imitate grassy forms and are extremely effective used here in association with ornamental grasses.

equally, leaving a central area along each side boundary. In one there is a seat and the other holds a superb copper water fountain that is the focus of the garden. The wall opposite the house, at the end of the central axis, has no strong feature but a line of five tall, slim ballerina crab apples fill the bed that runs along it, with ground-covering *Waldsteinia ternata* below. The central space is clear enough for six people to dine. This is an example of traditional symmetry given a new twist.

a place to rest

The idea that gardens are for people to live in has been resurrected from Roman and classical times. In the past there was always provision made for pausing, to rest the walker or the horses. Seats were considerably placed where there would be a scenic view and often, in exposed parts of the garden, enclosure was necessary. Through the centuries places have been reserved for rest, like medieval turf seats that eventually gave way to sheltered arbours, graduating to splendid pavilions, Italian loggias, romantic gazebos, classical temples and exotic kiosks. By the nineteenth century, taking tea on the terrace had become routine.

the terrace Traditionally a terrace, firmly outlined by a balustrade, separated house from garden, but in the modern garden this would be regarded as ostentatious and divisive. Ornamental boundaries like this are unimportant now because, however formal, modern gardens are concerned with unity. So there is no replacement for the balustrade:

Instead, the paved edges may be concealed by plants that blur the perimeter of the hard landscaping, linking it with the garden. In some cases this can mean bringing even formally clipped plants right into the paving, as can be seen in the garden illustrated on page 126.

Paved areas no longer exist only to set the house well but must also meet the needs of those who will spend time there. Consequently the paving is not necessarily adjacent to the house but may be at the far end of the garden. Even if it is next to the house, it may not be parallel to it but angled towards sunlight, say at 45 degrees. The convenience of the sitter is of more importance than the dignity of the building. Many modern designs use the diagonal (see plan on page 95) because it maximizes space, and makes interesting garden areas that are not symmetrical but have a strongly formal underlying geometry. The dynamic of the garden no longer lies ahead, at 90 degrees to the house, but leads to side areas as discussed in the previous chapter.

In the town, the terrace has given way to the smaller patio. Many modern gardens are now enclosed, inward-looking courtyards. These may be gravelled for sun-loving plants but will have paving inset for seating and a table. Sundecks are perfect for warm areas and false levels of no more than 70–100mm (3–4in) are easily put in to add interest. Formality is always inherent in decking because it is a linear medium.

seats Today it would be unthinkable that seating is not a priority concern of the garden owner. Whether permanent or temporary, seats

Seating is always more welcoming when set against a boundary. In a garden designed by Bonita Bulaitis, huge panels of blue crushed glass set in resin create a fan-like back to the moulded wooden bench on steel legs. The soft textures of the surrounding plants flow into a pink bonded-gravel surface whose blue-painted lines echo the glass panels.

Here the 'traditional' features of a formal garden – pergola, trellis and obelisks – are made of metal and wire mesh. Their appearance is deliberately left stark, without plants that would soften and conceal their construction. But lavenders, aromatic herbs and grasses, hazy with flowers, add softening textures to the garden at ground level.

are planned in from the start as part of the formality. The fitted garden is an entirely modern idea and, where space is really limited, it enables the owner to have built-in seating, raised planting troughs and a small water feature, with storage space below for garden tools. Even the table may be part of the fitted units (see photograph on page 43). Heavy-duty timber makes an inexpensive version of this but a concrete frame could be clad with expensive sealed limestone for a cleanly elegant look.

Though functional, seating should have an aesthetic role as well. This could mean commissioning an inventive piece of seat-sculpture. It can

below *Julia Brett designed this compact courtyard to hold a tall sculpture of burnished steel by Simon Percival. It is set centrally in the sunken 'well' of the courtyard, where it can be viewed from all three floors of the house.*

116

simply be a matter of building bench seats and table, with Shaker simplicity, as part of the lines of the design. There could be some individualist pieces that can be moved around the site, like people, adding quirkiness and style wherever they go. Or their design may be strong enough to provide the sculptural focus of the garden.

summer houses Enclosed seating areas are made to provide shelter from sun, wind or rain and they have been ingenious in the past. Today the term 'summer house' encapsulates wooden circular or octagonal shelters (see photograph on page 110), often covered with trellis and smothered with climbers; smooth painted timber buildings with a transparent wall; concrete and glass buildings with sliding doors; and polycarbonate 'glasshouses', possibly on a turntable so that they may follow the sun. Many of these summer houses have storage space at the back, being true to the modern ethic of function linked with design. None of these is rustic but they are designed with geometric form and without fussy decoration. In a lighter touch revived from the past, wirework has reappeared. It is now less fancy, with no lace-like arabesques or central finials, but is stronger, made by weaving and wrapping wire around a heavy metal frame.

pergolas, arches and arbours
Arbours were originally shaded seats with plants trained over them. They were partially enclosed, wrapped on either side by a timber vine-clad frame that continued overhead, ensuring privacy and offering protection from both midday sun and chilling winds. They became extended so that, by the late fifteenth century, long tunnels had developed, also covered by twining or trained plants. These usually followed the perimeter of the garden, rather like cloisters, offering views into the central pleasure garden as the visitor progressed around the site. Later these densely shaded tunnels gave way to the light-dappled pergolas we know today.

Today the pergola as a walkway is still much in evidence. To progress along a garden with a view on both sides harks back to the symmetrical approach, but if a pergola runs on one side of the garden only an evergreen boundary hedge can force attention the other way, into the light and space of the garden. In this case very little greenery should cover these posts so that the scene is not obscured. Although pergola

above **This huge linked monolithic sculpture by Jack Lenor Larson emphasizes the scale of the lake and woodland beyond by massive concrete and metal frames that dwarf the people-space below.**

opposite below **In a stylish suburban garden a square pergola made of heavy timber beams is supported by classical columns and has no need of climbing plants.**

walks should be intimate they should also be wide and tall enough for comfort. So a really tall (2.5m/8ft high) pergola will allow trailing racemes such as wisteria flowers from above and a similar width will enable you to grow a line of small plants inside the length of the walkway, such as *Heuchera* 'Red Spangles' or spring crocus followed by tall, slim alliums.

Arches are freestanding but may be used to unite structures like walls and fences, continuing the line while allowing access through them. They are also used to draw attention to places of partition, where one area finishes and another begins, like the transition from flower garden to sitting area. Today arches may be treated as tantalizing sculpture, spaced at intervals or solo, often huge and usually without plants. They might frame a view or simply act as a witty focal point. Recent developments in

Artificial mist rolls along the ground as if it were early morning in winter in this sensuous garden at Chaumont sur Loire, France. Diamond-woven trellis makes compartments like side chapels in a cathedral.

the modern garden use overhead beams as structural reinforcement of the design. These freestanding beams lead into the garden space, confirming the formal geometry and defining the spaces below, while adding a three-dimensional element to the garden's geometry. They do not always have to be covered with plants.

Pergolas were, and still are, often made from a series of iron hoops, so that the arches were curved overhead, otherwise from lengths of timber with flat rafters and beams supported by timber posts or brick piers. In the modern formal garden timber is still used but it is never rustic. The posts are not elaborately grooved, there are no fussy finials and the rafters are plain edged, rather than curvaceous. Classical pillars, so loved by the Victorians, are out unless there is deliberate witty intent.

Tubular steel posts sometimes replace timber uprights, or concrete posts stand in for the original fancy brick piers. Painting or staining makes these structures look softer.

Steel, aluminium and bent bamboo canes are new suitable materials for flat or rounded pergolas, with recycled and economic bolted scaffolding as an increasingly popular alternative. Overhead protection suggests additional materials, supported by the crossbeams. Strengthened glass or panels of transparent polycarbonate protect from rain and canvas canopies will protect from bright light and heat. If you have patience, living tunnels may be grown on the principle of pleaching, by planting laburnum, hornbeam or lime trees, which bend well, in rows on opposite sides of a path and manipulating them from clear stems until they form an arched tunnel.

water

Every period of garden history has involved water in some way and it is just as important in the modern garden, where it is almost always seen as an artistic feature, rather than an allusion to landscape. All the ideas of the past are still popular, though now scaled down. The famous fountains of the Villa d'Este were powered by gravity, but far smaller equivalents today depend on electric pumps. Once, water played over marble or rock, but modern alternatives are verdigris-ed copper, slate, stainless steel or glass. Large waterfalls may no longer gush down in free fall but instead may trickle gently from one stepped, smooth surface down to another. And rills can now flow around the garden space rather than becoming its central axial line.

Water can be made to do extraordinary things. We are familiar with fountains, spouts, falls, canals and rills, and most of the modern adaptations of these are described in the chapter on minimalist gardens (see page 141), but there are also new ideas made possible by technology that have caused a frisson in modern gardens. One of these creates an element of surprise in a formally organized setting, when mist appears suddenly, to drift around the site. This involves a technique using liquid nitrogen mixed with air to vaporize. It is passed along pipework and a fan blows it through into the chosen part of the garden. Such a feature depends upon a modern timer, making the mist appear and disappear at prearranged times. Sometimes a refrigerator processor is fitted in to keep the mist close to the ground.

sculpture

Often the functional elements chosen for a garden, be it a water feature or a piece of furniture, are so well formed and interesting in themselves that they attract attention immediately, in which case any other sculpture would be superfluous. But sculpture has been a feature of gardens since

119

A trough of dark water brings the light of the sky down to ground level in this garden of linear design by Tom Sitta. Sparely planted black bamboos run parallel to the water, to be reflected in its surface.

Reminiscent of the parterres of old, herbs like chives and variegated horseradish are displayed in the centre of box-framed planting beds contained by concrete paving.

Roman times and today it plays an increasingly popular role, providing a focus and adding a distinctive and personal note to a garden.

When selecting a piece there are many considerations and to complete the formally modern style of the garden you need to make decisions about the size of the piece, whether it is to be dramatic or gentle and whether you prefer figurative or abstract work. The latter particularly opens up a vast choice of materials, from slate to glass, to cast plastics and metals, fibreglass and wood. The modern formal garden is not the place for a half-size classical goddess, unless the intention is to amuse. However, this does not mean that figurative art should be rejected – contemporary art is not always abstract. There are some beautiful figures that will establish a presence in the garden, and be

pleasing all year, but they must be in scale with the site and express the spirit of the garden. In the past, work was often displayed imposingly on a tall plinth, deliberately impressive, and maintaining a distance between viewer and 'art'. Today's preference is for pieces to be more accessible by placing them at ground level.

Siting is very important. Is the work to be revealed or hidden? A piece may be deliberately over-large, in which case no one will notice anything else, or there could be several linked small pieces, sited as subtle detail, to be 'happened upon' mysteriously around a corner or near a seating area. You may provide the perfect backcloth, such as a panel of luminous, laminated, pitted glass to silhouette the form, or a clipped niche in rigid pyracantha, rather like cathedral sculpture. If the work is to be viewed from all around, it should be freestanding and not placed at the end of a vista. Bear in mind that some sculpture is static and tranquil while other work may be stirring or exciting, in which case rustling tall bamboo or a wall of rippling vines, like *Parthenocissus henryana*, provides an appropriate setting.

If professionally made work is beyond your means, monolithic pieces of rock or timber make simple but effective sculpture for the modern formal garden. Or consider organic found objects as described on page 56, or recycled industrial pieces that soften with a velvet coating of red rust. Careful lighting considerably enhances both, either as spots or silhouettes, and note that sculpture is often tied in closely with water as part of the whole feature (see photograph on page 131).

clipped features

Hedging has always been used to define area: small or tall, hedges are gentler than walls. Low hedges were grown to create smaller partitions like parterres and mazes but over time their popularity waned, whenever nature was seen to be more significant than design, as in the eighteenth

century at the time of Capability Brown. But then a revival would follow as the next generation became intrigued by a less recent past and formal gardens were in fashion again. Today clipping is very much back in vogue, partly because, since the plants are evergreen, a hedge looks the same all year round and also because this is gardening at its most obedient.

hedges Hedges were an ancient means of enclosure and from its rural beginnings the formal hedge quickly became the norm in gardens. Their function was still important but the design potential was quickly realized. Clipped hedges, like those described in Part 1 (see page 64), are used widely in the modern garden because they can define geometry with three-dimensional precision. In the contemporary garden no one has used hedging to experiment with formal space better than the Belgian garden designer Jacques Wirtz, whose calm green gardens link house with paved area, in total harmony with the enclosed, dramatically foliaged plants. Today hedges may meander in organic curves, converge on a single point where a sculpture is sited or be planned like café curtains, screening the street yet at the same time revealing the view. Pierced openings in these garden divisions are made dramatic by the play of light and shadows.

parterres Low on the ground, parterres were planted to edge beds of herbs or flowers. Designs were originally simple, mostly straight lines, but soon the knot garden came into fashion with its scrolls and woven ribbon-like patterns. These were described as 'parterres de broderie', which shows the thinking behind them – embroidered flat patterns. The new interest in parterres stems from our perception of the garden as a space with atmosphere into which we may step, appreciating the practical fact that the garden always looks well groomed.

Elaborate knots and parterres are no longer used for two-dimensional pattern making but provide the structure of garden spaces or act as living sculpture. They may still be low but they have now become a series of enclosures, each with a sense of space that is as important as the hedge itself. And this is particularly evident at night when the modern parterre is enhanced by garden lighting, revealing open spaces, shadowed areas and the mass of the solid forms enclosing them.

In early morning light metal-framed sculptures, set against a timber-clad house, drip with tangled plants. Below, parallel runs of dwarf box are planted in organically meandering lines.

with complicated parterres. Eventually a three-dimensional element was brought in to add to the fun because tall hedges effectively blindfolded the visitor. Puzzle mazes are a great feature of gardens all over Europe and endure today as a source of entertainment. The current revival of interest in mazes seems to be less ornamental and more because mazes are ambiguous, adding an air of mystery to a garden. And however formal the modern garden may be, it is desirable that it is not only a thing of beauty but a place that touches the spirit and has atmosphere.

Some mazes are flat and cut out of turf as in the past, while others may just be a pattern of paviours on the ground. Whatever the intention, they suit the simplicity and clarity of the highly organized modern garden and should be accurately planned on paper. It is easiest to use geometry – including straight lines, parts of circles, chicanes, dead ends and ultimately a 'centre', that need not be in the centre. However they are made, what matters is the sense of challenge in pursuit of the goal.

topiary If shrubs and turf can be manipulated for art, then topiary is the ultimate freestanding living sculpture in-the-round. The same craftsmanship learned in past gardens has been revived today for several reasons. One is that, like Everest, topiary is always there and modern gardens, having become outdoor rooms, are not just for summer. Another reason is the practical realization that, once formed, topiary is easy to manage. But it is also a fact that the same quality applies to topiary as to many manifestations of modern gardens, in that it brings back a sense of the spirit of place, so beloved by William Kent.

The folksy fun with peacocks, chickens and even teddy bears has passed and gardeners now want something more sophisticated. Simple mathematical forms like cubes, cones, wedges and spheres have a static presence in the garden space and create an air of mystery. Purely abstract forms have been made recently, based on rolling landscape or crowding boulders, which link with 'land art', a contemporary type of landscaping. This is when the land is shaped on the scale of a Neolithic monument to create a new art of landscape, as practised in North America and the likes of the famous Garden of Cosmic Speculation in Scotland, devised by Charles Jencks and Maggie Keswick.

Topiary 'sculptures' look ageless but can be planned easily and at no great expense. As they grow from the ground, you must have a clear

To make a parterre today, aim at a very simple framework and decide whether you want flowing curves and open areas or prefer boxed-in geometric spaces. Do not feel you should fill every space with plants. Some parts may be paved for sitting, others hold sculpture but many could be left pleasingly empty. The garden will have an atmosphere in all seasons – frosted, freshly greened or shadowy in the dark. Evergreen box was mostly used for parterres in the past, or occasionally grey-leaved lavender or santolina. Today a deciduous enclosure could be made of low-growing plants such as thrift (*Armeria maritima*), chives (*Allium schoenoprasum*) or lilyturf (*Liriope muscari*).

mazes The maze has new life. Its riddle appears to stretch back to times before records were made. Possibly the old maze drawings inscribed on rock faces were an attempt to represent the mysteries of the spirit life, but they continue to fascinate because those same mysteries are still with us. From small drawings larger labyrinths evolved and by the middle of the Dark Ages these took the form of turf mazes, cut out of flat ground, consisting of single routes that wrapped around a central desired objective. Possibly processional in origin, these eventually became no more than ornamental 'teasers' that had strong visual links

opposite *Symmetry almost – but not quite – rules this whimsical garden of gnome-like topiary. Traditionally inspired, but entirely modern, at the central 'crossing' a pyramid faces a dome-topped cube in dynamic confrontation, like the showdown in a game of chess.*

below *The 'patte d'oie' was a system of radiating paths popular in seventeenth-century France. Here the idea has been translated on a small scale by Marc Schoellen, with soft beech hedges that lead to a meadow.*

layout in mind; this is essential if the garden is to be hard paved. Gravel could be considered as a good basis, but not grass that needs mowing. For shrubs that lend themselves to clipping, refer to Part 1 (page 64). Like sculpture, you may choose to place them symmetrically where they flank a path or plan them as a highly distinctive focus, like asymmetric 'cloud topiary' (see page 68). Topiary can also be grown in containers and moved around to suit the mood, but fit castors to make this easier. A mass of small, geometrically shaped topiary, say pyramids and cones, could fill a courtyard, leaving only the sitting area empty. A strong statement like this would need no other plants, apart from the greening of the boundaries.

flow garden

This intimate area of a large country garden, between house and river, has been designed
as a special place with the intention of linking the two. The author, with Barbara Hunt,
planned the spacious sweep of terrace, edged with wide, low box, to link with the flow of
plants. The same slow curves are followed with interweaving runs of flat coursed bricks and
soft santolina and lavender varieties, with small grassy day lilies (*Hemerocallis*). Seasonally
effective perennials, from tulips through to colourful, summer-flowering species and late-
season grasses, merge with the flowing paths. The strong forms of clipped yews, characteristic
of the locale, radiate from the house, enclosing but also drawing the visitor into the great
lawn. Light pierces the gaps, moving slowly across the plants during the day.

top **Bound gravel and random paving follow the 'flow'
theme, with a flat run of bricks crossing the path. Ceramic
sculptures by Veronique Maria, with small stipas and
double red helianthemums, mark out a transition area.**

above **Detail shows the textures and form of the selected
plants. Santolina and lavender establish permanent
shaping while the infilling with seasonally changing
plants includes Knautia macedonica, Stipa gigantea,
Sedum spectabile and the tall globes of alliums.**

concepts

One of the greatest aspects of progress during the twentieth century is
that diversity and personality in all the arts flourished, which is why no
two modern gardens ever look alike. A formal approach still means order
and unity but it should not crush individual flair. The belief that great
gardens need a soul still holds true for the modern garden and in new
formal designs based around a concept, the spirit of place is brought
together with the order of re-invented geometry, releasing the
uniqueness of the plot and giving life to the garden.

In practice this means that all the spatial divisions and chosen plants
work better when there is a clear design concept for the site. In a well-
planted garden this may be a simple matter of working with the climate
and conditions and accepting no foreigners. The English woodland
garden could be the inspiration, for example. Beneath a tree canopy, low
layers of ferns, hellebores, spurge and woodrush flourish in the dappled
light. In the midst of this could be a treasured open square, a grassed
glade containing plants like English bluebells, cranesbills, primulas and
violets. The layout could be formalized in a domestic garden, with small
trees planted in a double line completely enclosing a perfectly square
central opening, the 'glade'. Solid wooden timbers might define the
edges and double up to make bench seats, with a fitted table in one
corner. The same timbers, laid flat, could provide an access path from
the house to the central square, with the ends running into planting.

Concepts also arise from respect for the atmosphere of a site and its
surroundings, such as a xeriscape garden, planned for water conservation
in an arid climate. A garden in California, designed by Isabelle Greene,
captures the essence of a hot, dry sloping site by building into it a series
of shallow concrete terraces, inspired by rice paddies, which impose a
structure on the garden (see photographs on pages 72 and 127). They
have been bewitchingly filled with drought-tolerant plants of texture and
colour, like tamarisk, water-retaining aloes and agaves, and spiky yuccas
and dasylirion. The spaces and lines of the garden are as sharply irregular
as the terrain and fit well with the stark modernity of the house.

In the country garden I designed in partnership with Barbara Hunt
(see also page 124), the concept arose from a slow flow of clear water
that came from an adjacent watercress farm; the water maintains a
constant level as it meanders through the large garden. Working with

125

the uniqueness of the site, we designed a 'flow garden' of winding fine gravel paths and a double row of coursed bricks, sinuously wending their way among serpentine planting. The planting, in widely sweeping organic curves, echoes the currents of slow-moving water.

History is the source of the conceptual gardens made by English designer George Carter (see photographs on pages 69, 104 and 111). They refer back to a time before the huge landscape movement of the eighteenth century, when formality ruled and gardens were self-contained places, ornamented by sculpture and seats. His clearly structured gardens often use symmetry, crossed by other axial lines

The curve of the terrace is edged with wide, low box from which mounds of plants echo the concept of flowing water. Santolina, artemisia and lavender, interspersed with day lilies, ornamental grasses and Heuchera 'Green Ivory', flow across the path, seen on the left. Buttresses of yew will be clipped into strong geometric wedge shapes when they are more mature.

leading to alcoves, each with a sculptural focus, or apertures that invite people into other areas. The grand manner is adapted for smaller spaces by playing with scale and by planning in a bold, decisive manner. There is always an air of mystery in his gardens, a feeling of suspended time, sometimes almost melancholia, but they are enriched by ornamental details that fill niches, augment straight lines and reinforce the sense of enclosure. Motifs belonging to a golden age of European grand design are intrinsic parts of the unity, so there are obelisks, finials, sun-golden spheres, classical statuary, and stretches of contained water that reflect light. None of this is sentimental reproduction. All the imagery is old but the gardens are modern in scale, materials and layout, creating a meditative, tranquil atmosphere.

So modern formality has also become a vehicle for self-expression. In the smaller town courtyard, your own sense of place may be created by making a totally green enclosure in an urban environment, with only textures allowed to enliven the scene. The lines of the layout could be established with different levels of clipped hedging and walls clad with neatly sheared pyracantha. Turf or chamomile seats, typical of medieval gardens, would suit the theme, while a square of silvery water could reflect the foliage of a small tree overhead, like *Sorbus cashmiriana*, a graceful tree with fine ferny foliage.

Humour was present in the great formal gardens – for example in the water spouts devised to emerge and spray the unwary visitor, or the musical organs created by the natural power of water at the Villa d'Este – and wit is part of the modern scene too. Another trend today is to play with scale, to offer the unexpected (see page 117). By using illusion and jokes, it is possible to make a garden that has endless potential for witty additions as time goes by. Consider using false perspectives that appear to lengthen the garden by tapered lines, narrowing pools and massive leaves like those of the hardy banana (*Musa basjoo*); spouts of water, as in the past, or vapour may be put on a timer to appear unexpectedly. A maze could be constructed with shallow water channels replacing hedges, so the path can be followed with obvious penalties for cheating. Or there could be a still pool that reflects the underside of a plain feature like a wide 'diving board', revealing its underside to have hidden depths. It would be interesting to build a huge, well-'buttressed' metal arch to show what wisteria can really do. Gardening can get too serious.

The proximity of the sea inspired the idea for this beach garden, so the borders are filled with bands of sea-washed bleached pebbles, interspersed with clipped santolina and purple sage, protected by a low windshield of woven willow.

Terraces resembling rice paddies make good use of a sloping site. Well-chosen plants thrive in this arid garden designed by Isabelle Greene (seen also on page 72).

At the start of a new century, we have to make realistic choices for our gardens. We have a deep respect for the wilderness, but people with busy lives want private garden spaces that do not make too many demands. Those who have little time to cope with uncontrolled natural bounty will choose a simple, elegant design. An outdoor space planned on minimally formal principles can be achieved relatively easily and its maintenance can be as minimal as its design. The idea of the minimalist garden arose from twentieth-century modernist architecture. Geometric buildings of unadorned concrete and glass planned on spare lines called for the adoption of a similar approach for the surrounding outdoor space. Such refinement need not be prohibitively expensive and, for the weary, this style of garden can be soothingly tranquil.

Within a walled building, open to the sky, a monoculture of moss is the minimalist theme. Mounds of grey-green moss are seen in low light that penetrates through the arches, filtered by a run of bamboo.

In any area of design, minimalism is the perfection of simplicity, the reduction to essentials, without ornamentation or excess. And the minimal garden is intrinsically formal, in that the order of lines and spaces is the governing factor upon which it is planned. These should be clearly defined, balancing the importance of utilitarian areas with the rest of the garden. An analytical approach like this involves straightforward planning, omitting any decoration that might distract from the unity of the whole. Open space is just as important as line and is in many ways the most significant feature of modern gardens. In a restless world, uncluttered openness is soothing and, indeed, has great beauty, provided nothing is allowed to distract from its seamless perfection.

For the space to succeed as a garden, there must be a focus, a place for the eye to rest – which could be a sculpture, a dramatic plant or a view beyond the boundaries. Its integrity also depends on the use of immaculate materials that harmonize rather than contrast and plants that remain relatively unchanged by the passage of time. Control is an essential feature and the garden's management should pay great attention to detail, always giving the appearance of effortless elegance.

practical matters

For many, the minimalist garden is a means of expressing delight in the elegance of judgement that a mathematician finds in a pleasing theorem or a musician in the niceties of harmony. It offers beautiful, simple style with a coherence of function and spirit that perfectly suits the mood of the new century. But such refinement means rigorous planning so that plants, features and materials are in accord, rather like the discipline of team sports, in which all individuals pull together with a single goal in mind. This approach should help you to resist impulsive purchases from a garden centre that would interrupt the balance of the garden as a whole.

cost

It is often assumed that minimal style means expensive and, indeed, such refinement can be costly. For example, if you choose materials like marble or limestone, steel or glass, not only are they relatively expensive but you will need professional advice about laying them. But with judicious choice of materials and careful planning, formal minimalism need not be out of reach. As described in Part 1 (see page 22), concrete is often an

minimally formal

top *The studiously placed line of three plant containers, like the three chairs facing the pool, define the outline of the limestone-paved terrace, without fuss.*

above *Fleeting shadows and a single tree provide the main detail in this courtyard of simple geometry.*

acceptable alternative to natural stone and, like gravel, is inexpensive to lay as well as providing the unity essential to minimally formal style. By incorporating a small amount of some more costly materials like bands of slate or slim strips of steel, the finished look is enriched. You should not economize on timber, however, because time alters it – cheap wood will warp and change colour. The most reliable timber for decks is Western red cedar (see page 28).

Solid boundaries enclosing the minimalist courtyard should be chosen with the same care. Synthetic materials are affordable and can be effective, like rendered and painted breeze blocks, the simple wash of colour on the wall becoming the perfect background for plants and features. Transparent screening that allows light through but ensures seclusion could be made from expensive stainless steel mesh panels but wide slats of timber set vertically, like a Venetian blind on its side, or polycarbonate panels in a wooden frame are more attainable and equally suited to minimal formality. Metals need not be luxurious either: scaffolding is simple to erect and, if recycled and painted, is also cheap.

As regards plants for a minimal garden, you will often need to 'buy time' in order to create an instant mature look. Clipped hedging, particularly box and yew, can set the scene immediately. It is possible to save money by buying small and watching them grow – but you will then have to wait for your garden to acquire the sense of permanence that is a feature of minimal formality. It is the same with specimen plants - it may be worth choosing a large dicksonia or fan palm, as described in Part 1 (see page 70), to establish the garden's focus in the first year. The consolation is that few plants are required for this style of garden.

maintenance

One of the chief objectives of choosing a minimal style of garden is that it should not demand too much of your time – and yet it is expected to be pristine all year. A simple maintenance programme should be planned from the start. Dirt and algae, possibly moss, will mark absorbent stone like limestones and sanstones, but professional pressure cleaning every year will restore it to an immaculate standard. Harder stone like marble or slate will stay unmarked if brushed regularly and washed occasionally (bear in mind that they are slippery when wet). Painted concrete will wear and need repainting but stained concrete should hold its colour. If aggregates are set into concrete, brushing and scrubbing are easily done.

Loose gravel is more difficult to keep clean unless all the plants are evergreen. Once laid, gravel is impossible to brush, so leaves must be picked up by hand. But if the gravel is set in resin (see page 24), brushing it clear is easy. Re-staining or painting a wooden deck is a chore but Western red cedar, which mellows to a silvery grey, needs no treatment.

Most walls need little regular maintenance apart from unpainted concrete, whose chic purity can be marked by deposits or weathering, if it is not sealed, making annual cleaning necessary. Everything that

A sculptural glass panel embellished with a geometric pattern intersects a pond and masks the entrance to the house. The courtyard, designed with elegant clarity, is animated only by wall shadows of bamboo and by the water that slides down the brimming bronze-edged pool. This is a detail of the garden designed by Ron Herman, shown on page 90.

far left *Light and shade are important in many minimalist gardens, as seen here where the strong lines of the pergola cast shadows on to the walls and floor. Texture is present in the linear floor patterns made from pebbles outlined by bands of concrete.*

left *Behind a simple seat, the expansion joint in the smooth cream concrete wall makes a strong line that is part of the design and, in a sun-filled space, allows the potential for shadows to be fully exploited.*

132 adheres to a concrete wall, like clinging plants, makes it difficult to repair or repaint. So the boundaries of a minimalist garden are often left bare, which suits the mood. If this is too austere for you, a wall of rippling green ivy makes a soft permanent backing that costs little and needs trimming at most twice a year.

Most evergreens need little attention so the main architectural plants could be a large, glossy-leaved *Magnolia grandiflora* or *Fatsia japonica*. Clipped plants will stay in dense, sharply defined health if clipped to a routine that you could mark in your diary – for example, yew once a year (in summer), box two or three times, *Lonicera nitida* and *Ligustrum jonandrum* about five times a year. Watering is a regular requirement: if the garden is small you can do it by hand, but in larger spaces it might be worth putting in an automatic irrigation system on a timer.

suitable materials

In minimally formal gardens, where the open space is more significant than any feature, the flooring materials become a flawless part of the garden's concept. But a garden that is designed on spare lines, textured or coloured only by the material from which it is made, can be almost severe. Therefore much depends on the materials you choose. They will often dictate the shape or layout of the space, just as coiled clay once influenced the basic form of Neolithic pottery.

It is important that unity at ground level is not spoiled by too much pattern. All paving, however small the units, looks best if the jointing is crisply perfect and the expanse is uninterrupted by too much contrasting colour and texture. Rectangular flagstones should ideally be butt-jointed (see page 18). A run of white marble, limestone or pale sandstone has a light-reflecting purity, making these immaculate materials perfect for minimal gardens. They can, however, be simulated by concrete flagstones like those described in Part 1 (see page 21), or replaced by simply textured, brushed concrete slabs. Small-unit paving, like blue-black stable pavers or dark clay tiles, also serve a minimal-style garden well, unifying the area by repetition so that the integrity of the design lies in the whole rather than the individual units. A continuous, uninterrupted flooring of painted or polished concrete that develops an attractive patina, or more sophisticated resin-bonded aggregates, are also true to the minimalist philosophy, the former being considerably more economic than the latter.

Hard surfaces like galvanized steel decking or stainless steel grid panels characterize 'high tech' minimalism, the style that uses industrial materials for an uncompromisingly modern effect. They are strikingly

The ocean is the focus here and detail therefore simplified in this exposed roptop garden designed by Topher Delaney. Clipped mounds of the drought-resistant grass Koeleria cristata *grow out of massed grey sedum at ground level, and a low-growing windproof pine in a square planter makes a shapely feature. The stylish metal mesh boundary filters the wind so there is little turbulence.*

clean-looking and practical for providing non-slip walkways and steps over water. But such metals are not suitable for a garden exposed to heat and both their cost and that of their construction are expensive. Dark engineering bricks look appropriate with metals because they too are precision-made. But wood could also be used, as a gentle contrast.

Softer flooring materials include timber decking, grass, rubber matting or rolled crumbed rubber in resin, all of which can cover the whole floor (see pages 22-8). Rubber surfaces are silent, so suit a formal atmosphere; choose subdued or neutral colours for a sympathetic effect. Smoothly sanded wood is also a soft and quiet surface and the lines of a deck will reinforce those of the design. Grass is a perfect carpeting medium

*The space is uncompromisingly divided up by
the solid rendered concrete walls in this minimal garden
designed by Steve Martino, but mimosa petals are
deliberately allowed to texture the smooth, slow water
of a raised pool. The flow of water is fed by a pipe set
in the dark wall visible through the gap.*

provided it is well-maintained: choose the finer lawn grasses and cut it regularly to maintain a bowling-green finish (though preferably without mown lines, which take control too far).

Mix materials with caution for minimalist appeal by avoiding dramatic extremes. Colour contrast is too strong for this type of garden but two different textures can be effective. Concrete may be softened by using a double line of naturally coloured stone setts as jointing in a smooth, light grey expanse. And for truly tactile softness, heavy lengths of timber can be laid slightly below the level of grass.

Elegantly and minimally formed, yellow kniphofias grow parallel to the slim steel railings in this balcony garden designed by Topher Delaney.

Boundaries work most effectively if they are similar to the flooring, creating continuity and therefore harmony. Concrete (see page 22) can copy almost any floor texture but if it looks too heavy, glass bricks have a luminous transparency that lightens the appearance of the garden while harmonizing by texture with most other materials and avoiding colour contrast. They blend with and illuminate solid rendered walls, letting light through. Slits in a high solid wall do the same, allowing spears of light to create moving floor patterns through the day. If some pattern is wanted, for example with mosaic or paint, make an even, 'all-over' effect on the concrete that will not distract attention from the garden's main focus.

using texture

Minimally formal gardens need not be arid because they conform to the ethic of simplicity and texture is a valuable means of creating character where there may be none. As described in Part 1, the range of paving materials is wider than ever (see page 16) but restraint is the key, so the number is best limited to two. Coarse textures are bold and add drama, while smooth textures suggest sophistication and glossy textures luxury.

Contrast is always exciting, so use texture for contrast, like a circle of coarse granite setts with smooth sandstone pavers, or noisy gravel beside quiet timber decking. Other ideas include warm wood with cold stone and immaculate slate with gritty crushed glass. Using textures that are similar in place of contrast is more subtle. The design can use textural subtlety as its elegant reductional theme so that the materials become self-effacing, avoiding competition and thus emphasizing other features. Granite setts with granite flagstones or pea shingle with rounded cobblestones merge visually, leaving the eye to be drawn elsewhere.

light and colour

Natural light is the most influential element in garden design and some of the best examples of minimalist gardens are those in consistent brilliant sunlight, due to the country's latitude. The work of Luis Barragan, one of the most influential landscapers of the twentieth century, is set in the unrelieved illumination of Central America. Shadows, moving with the sun, provide animation that relieves the plainness of his painted concrete walls.

The difference in the quality of light between southern and northern Europe is borne out historically. The cathedrals of Italy have large areas of frescoed wall, with few windows, because the light is strong and the summer heat relentless, whereas in the great cathedrals of northern Europe, with its lower light levels, illuminated windows became the

135

Faced with a tall, overbearing brick wall partially enclosing a courtyard, this design brings light and warmth with cream-rendered walls and polished cream limestone flooring. The symmerical focus is a glassy weir falling from a letterbox slit in the red-painted panel in front of the arched wall niche. The evergreen planting of ivy, clipped box and Prunus laurocerasus 'Otto Luyken' tolerates shade.

dominant art. Because the light is less harsh in northern climates, every opportunity should be grasped to exploit it, making pierced walls, open wooden trellis, steel mesh panels and glass bricks appropriate features.

Colour is welcomed everywhere, though in minimalist gardens it is best if it is neither riotous nor sentimental. Instead neutral tones, dark tones or simple black or white are ideal. Natural, unpainted wood, sedimentary sandstones and sealed concrete are all neutral paving materials with muted colour – not simply monochrome, but with gradations according to the material. Harder metamorphosed stone like marble or slate can have comparatively strident streaks of mineral colour. The plainer forms of both suit modern formality best. A white-on-white philosophy is fitting, with green the only interruption in the form of foliage: such pristine spaces need to be regularly and rigorously managed.

In terms of plants, grey evergreens like the sword-leaved *Phormium tenax* or the brown ornamental grass *Carex buchananii*, along with the mahogany-coloured *Iris germanica*, have neutral colours that would grace a minimalist garden. Plants too may be chosen for black and white drama, such as white lilies emerging from a sea of black-leaved lilyturf (*Ophiopogon planiscapus* 'Nigrescens') in a silvery galvanized metal pot.

Applied colour in the form of paints and stains, as described in Part 1 (see page 22), may be used economically on either timber or concrete. Unless the stain is transparent, the base material can be less important in the garden than its colour. The earth colours of Roman times, such as ochre, are gently acceptable because they relate to the natural colours of plants and, as they merge so softly, they are welcome in all climates. However, stronger saturated colours may become the overriding theme of a minimalist garden, where such brilliance is suited to the unforgiving light of the sun, making both decoration and plant detail superfluous. Light and shade play upon intense colour, altering it during the day, so little else is needed. In the bluer light of Northern countries, strong colour needs careful handling but can revitalize a courtyard on a grey winter day.

the focus

No garden design should be so complicated so that the eye is unsure where to rest and the design of a minimalist garden, in particular, should be so elegantly devised that the eye is led instantly to the focus. Decide when planning where the focus will be – on a sight line from a window

top *A traditionally built house has been transformed by a minimal makeover. A glassed-in 'cloister' walkway looks into the elegantly simple internal courtyard created by architect Seth Stein. Neither planting nor ornament distract from its sophisticated geometry.*

above *Sentinels of cactus are the focus of an enclosure formed by orange-painted concrete walls, designed by Martha Schwartz. Square apertures pierce it with light.*

inspired symmetry

This minimally conceived urban garden, planned on symmetrical principles, is tiny but it manages to seat six people for an alfresco meal in summer. Because of its restricted size and the few key details, the space is kept simple, with everything in balance and planting that is easy to maintain.

The paving is made from slim, pale limestone flagstones, laid parallel with the house, its mortared jointing lines part of the design. Four tall clipped-yew buttresses, two on each side wall, reinforce the garden's symmetry and define the important spaces for permanent seating and the fountain.

The copper fountain, designed by Barbara Hunt, drips water from triangular containers into the catchment pool below. This focus is deliberately sited centrally on the side wall: placing it in the centre of the wall opposite the house would have decreased the 'depth' of this shallow garden. Instead, five really slim trees, Ballerina crab apples, planted along the far wall, emphasize the symmetry without creating a focus.

top **One splendid fan palm, Trachycarpus fortunei,** *is all that a minimal garden may need as a focus.*

above **The symmetrical layout of this small garden by George Carter creates a theatrical atmosphere. To the sides, theatrical 'wings' are formed using clipped Choisya ternata, while, centre stage, a pool and dark urn provide the focus.**

or as an unexpected surprise when entering the garden. The hidden lines of the garden will indicate a good position for the focus, always avoiding competition from other dominant features.

Any strong shape that is different from the surrounding horizontals and verticals will draw attention. In a large plot the traditional focus may be a specimen cedar upon a sweep of lawn, backed by clipped hedging, celebrating the beauty of something that would be only a detail in a busy garden. A well-placed seat, piece of sculpture or a multi-stemmed tree set in a small courtyard instantly draws attention. The focus could also be a group of similar objects or it may be the space between features that draws the eye (see page 79) or like a path between lines of hedging.

People need places to sit and spaces for plants, but both should be so well chosen that their form is a joy to see as well as to use. Seats commissioned from a sculptor are expensive but serve a dual role in a minimal garden, providing exciting form as well as seating. Or you could simply group together blocks of granite ordered from a stone mason, but this would also be costly. Fitted semi-circular seats made from concrete or solid timber would be a cheaper way of achieving the same effect.

Geometry need not control all the details of a minimally formal garden but it provides a perfect foil for contrasting organic forms, like man-made sculpture, naturally formed rock or, in a frost-free area, a gnarled olive tree. Because of their curvaceous form, oversized containers like huge clay oil jars are enough on their own, without plants, when they become sculptural features. Placed well into the depths of a garden, they will always draw the eye. Planted containers make other excellent foci. Suitable subjects include tall grasses, like the perennial *Miscanthus floridulus* (which reaches over 3m/10ft in summer, having been cut back in late winter) or single well-formed shrubs like the erect evergreen Japanese holly (*Ilex crenata* 'Fastigiata'). A group of containers may be placed so that they make a triangle, a square or a rank of identical plants.

As we have seen, size is one way of attracting attention and including a large sculpture in a small space can be dramatic. Commissioned sculpture is perfect for the chic formal garden but it is costly, so instead, consider using 'found' objects made from contrasting materials to attract the eye, provided this is in keeping with your pristine, minimalist space. In a Japanese-inspired garden, for example, you might have a naturally formed chunk of rock or attractive, weather-worn timbers (see page 56).

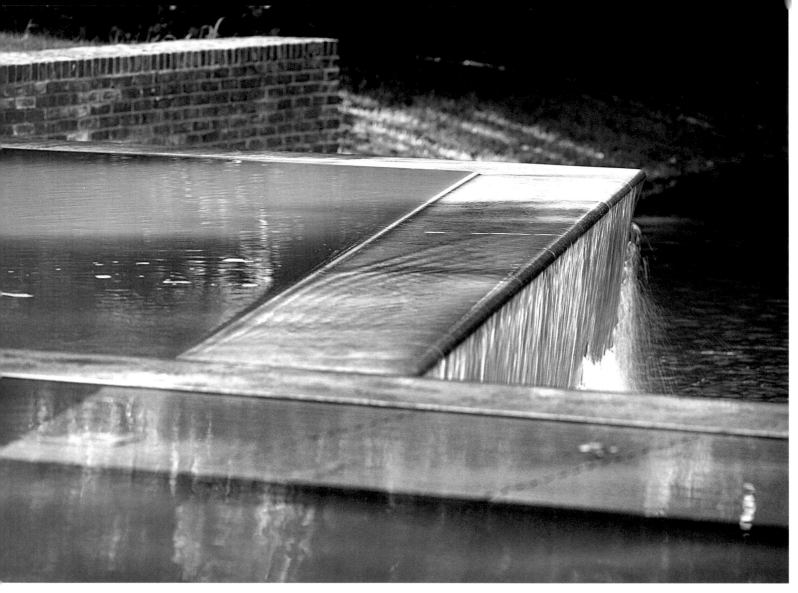

A wide coping stone with a rounded edge aids the smooth flow of water as it brims over to fall heavily into the pool below.

Sometimes it is the tension between plants or objects which carries the minimalist effect. One rock, for example, may be placed as an 'outlier', similar to and linked with a group, but apart, making the space between significant. The objects could equally be identical small trees, the tension between them carrying the minimalist theme. Because vertical forms always catch the eye, three fastigiate trees in different parts of a courtyard will relate strongly to one another, but it is the space in between where the eye will rest.

Plants themselves provide attention-grabbing forms that enliven
and provide a focus for the otherwise static minimalist courtyard.
One magnificent bamboo, like *Fargesia nitida*, whose canes reach
2–3m (6ft 6in–10ft), would be a star. Or the hardy fan palm (*Chamaerops
humilis*) suggests an exotic overtone. Plants with large foliage such as
the tree peony (*Paeonia delavayi* var. *ludlowii*) have matt, deeply incised
large leaves that are a fresh green in spring with the bonus of soft yellow,
poppy-like flowers. The evergreen, leathery glossy-leaved loquat tree
(*Eriobotrya japonica*) grown as a clipped evergreen lollipop would be
effective in a small space, unless the shade of a canopy, like that of
white-stemmed *Betula utilis* var. *jacquemontii*, is preferred. Multi-
stemmed trees as referred to in Part 1 are also ideal foci (see page 81).

Unless all plants are to be grown in deep containers, provision for
planted areas must be made in the formal layout of the flooring. Once
planted, it is not possible to dig below paving, so deep digging and the
addition of rich, moist organic matter will give plants a good start.

including water

Modern minimalist principles can be rather austere and even a small
quantity of water will enliven a garden designed on these lines.
A reflective pool, small or large, is soundless and sets a calm atmosphere
as well as bringing the sky down to floor level. Any flicker of movement,
like a gentle ripple that never breaks the surface, is revealed by light.

Flowing water is soothing. The sophisticated minimalist garden might
have water falling as a glassy, transparently smooth weir or gently guided
down angled slate or sheet steel as a slide. An immaculate water scheme
can become expensive if it needs professional expertise. But a small fall of
water can be built more economically so that it drops, transparently clear,
through a horizontal slit in a wall which conceals the pump (see page
48). To be sure the water falls free, fix a thin overhanging lip of smooth,
round-edged perspex, tile or slate along the slit, with a long groove on
the underside to prevent the water flowing back on to the wall.

Forcefully ejected water, such as jets spouting from the ground or
from a side wall, is dramatic and stirs the air. A single jet falling into a
circular pool makes a classically simple focus and is relatively inexpensive
to make. But a line or grid of such jets needs professional expertise
because of the required water pressure. The water can be collected into

*A thick slit in the wall of stainless steel has a projecting
metal lip to ensure that water falls clear of the wall,
making a transparent weir down to the pool below,
bordered on one side by a triangle of black* Ophiopogon
planiscapus *'Nigrescens'.*

141

a perimeter channel, covered by a grille, which takes it below ground into a reservoir to be recycled all over again, leaving no water on the surface.

When considering the quantity of water in one feature, bear in mind that noisy water can be irritating rather than soothing – and the heavier the flow, the louder it will be. But do not let this stop you from using fountains: if not too large, such schemes make simple and effective features of the minimalist garden. You will need to take advice on the means of water circulation and the choice of pump size. A timer can be set to regulate the display and the pump may be switched off at times.

The size of any water feature should be in scale with the space. Given this, the shape of a pool may be either circular or rectangular to fit with the geometry. A 'mini-canal', running the length of a small courtyard, should follow the design lines of the garden. Narrow rills, resembling those of Moorish gardens of the past, have a linear quality that complements the small minimalist garden. In a larger space, the idea can be expanded to include parallel rills with lines of dwarf bamboo between.

Raised water troughs can be built with very simple, wide coping that doubles as seating. This fits well in a small space, keeping other furniture to the minimum. But in larger, elegantly contemporary gardens raised pools may be designed so that brimming water is level with the sides, allowing for continuous overflowing. The effect is created by surface tension that makes water cling to the pool, then slide into a reserve channel on all sides to be recirculated.

The size of the water area will affect the cost. For small minimalist gardens there are affordable water features with small pumps in enclosed systems that recycle water. Examples include drilled rocks down which water trickles or a group of vertical metal tubes, each one spilling water. A silvery metallic sphere, permanently coated with a film of water, is another effective small feature. All water features must of course be leakproof and in the minimal garden such attention to detail is crucial. This is achieved by either building a concreted sealed base or lining a pool with purpose-made flexible plastic sheeting, like butyl (see page 53). The costs are similar and both systems reliable unless there is any possibility of the liner being pierced by rough handling. Joints should be carefully heat-sealed and all edges concealed from view by the overlap of the garden flooring. In sophisticated formal courtyards successful pools, filled to the brim, never show a low-water mark.

linking with the building

We have already seen that the concept of the minimalist garden arose from modernist architecture of the twentieth century, with its clean lines and new building materials. Its principle of functional, elegant simplicity is ideally suited to, and often associated with, small modern courtyards but it can be used successfully for other sizes and shapes of garden.

Designing gardens in a modern, chaste manner can be bedevilled by the associated building because not all of these will be beautifully simple. In reality the minimalist modern house and garden combined is something of a dream ticket. Many houses are old and for much of the last century their gardens emulated the large gardens of history, but often these do not scale down successfully and the result can look contrived. Building on this, modernism can be incorporated to a greater degree while some historical connections remain as a source of inspiration.

Laying out the garden is usually easier with a modern house, because the structure is clearly visible when the house is designed on simple, geometric principles. A major feature of modern buildings is large, plain windows which will link house and garden through the seasons with a transparency undreamed of in the past. Doors may slide wide, blending garden space with interior space. Choosing the same flooring for inside and out, such as limestone flags or clay tiles, further blurs the boundary line. The few plants should be strongly architectural to draw the eye. Garden partitions may echo internal ones by dividing the outdoor space in similar proportions, perhaps using dwarf box as a defining edge. Water too should be simple: a glassy weir would echo the glass of the house.

The problem of linking a modern, minimally formal style of garden with an older house can be resolved by developing lines, proportion and

opposite *Mixing the modern with the old can work effectively, as shown here where the simple geometry of flattened cobble paths relates to the 'random' pattern of the stone building. But the raked dark gravel infilling each rectangle shows a distinctly oriental influence, echoed by the young bamboos encircled by moss.*

This minimalist courtyard garden, designed by Seth Stein to suit the uncompromisingly modern architecture of the concrete-built house, uses white rounded cobblestones and a timber platform-table as the only contrasting textures. Modern adaptations of traditional themes include the plain concrete 'pavilion' on the roof and the verandah topped by louvred beams that reaches out into the garden space, managing light and shade below. The semi-transparent divide, made from a panel of opaque glass, affirms the link between house and courtyard.

japanese simplicity

This essentially simple design owes much to classical Japanese gardens. Sliding doors from the house open on to timber decking with planks of different widths. A clipped dome of red-flowered *Rhododendron* 'Hinode-giri', a Kurume hybrid azalea, is planted in the ground and tightly clipped to cover part of the deck. A path made of concrete aggregate slabs, infilled with small pebbles, leads to the L-shaped pool, a small variegated bamboo (*Pleioblastus viridistratus*) running along its length. Three concrete slabs lead over the water to a granite seat below *Rhododendron luteum*, a fragrant yellow-flowered azalea ultimately 4m (12ft) high. Beside the stepping stones, small *Typha minima* pick up the line of bamboo.

Fine gravel covers the rest of the garden, apart from the helxine (*Soleirolia soleirolii*) that greens its far end for much of the year, imitating moss. Its flowing shape is retained by a trim to stop spreading. The ground-level pool, edged with a stainless steel strip, is broken by a flat-topped rock that has a dynamic relationship with a twin, similar-sized rock, adding tension to the otherwise calm garden. The deep purple flowering *Clematis* 'Warsaw Nike', behind the second rock, is in colour when the rhododendrons are finished. In the pool three areas of red *Nymphaea* 'Froebelii' cover some of the water surface with lily pads. Below it, *Fontinalis antipyretica* oxygenates the water.

scale that are sympathetic to the existing building (see the photograph on page 137). Ignore ornamental details and let the 'bones' of the house structure provide the format for the garden layout. You may pick up the width of the windows and entrances, taking lines from the house at right angles and establishing proportions that relate to both. Cross these with lines parallel to the house to form sympathetic spaces that become the garden's framework. Many of these 'lines' will not be visible, but linked plants and features, placed in relation to them, acknowledge underlying structure. Ideally, the materials used should match those of the house, but many old houses are brick and brick is not the best paving material for a minimalist space, associated as it is with rural and romantic gardens.

Choose an area in sunlight for sitting and divide the remaining space with lines, displayed or hidden, clearly delineating an area for eating, an area for plants and one for an uninterrupted view. Anything extraneous – like garden equipment, extra seats, empty containers – should be hidden from view, perhaps by a false wall or by a small building in line with the design. Bear in mind the value of open space and leave it clear of detail. There is no need to fill it with flowers, tubs, seats or patterns because it is a pleasure in itself, implying freedom and room to move. Like a glade in a wood, space relaxes the spirit. Plain surfaces emphasize the uncluttered style but formally planned lines of plants, such as clipped box hedging or a row of evergreen *Liriope muscari*, can define spaces. The crucial focus can be a simple feature at the end of an invisible line.

roof gardens

Being off the ground means being closer to the sky, the light and the elements. No architectural style need influence the design so, given such a free hand and bearing in mind weight constraints, a roof garden becomes an ideal candidate for uncluttered minimalism.

Consult a structural engineer before devising the plan for a rooftop. The strongest load-bearing areas of the floor will normally be around the perimeter or above structural beams inside the building. The frame to support a floor can be fixed over these and this is where to site planted containers, leaving the central area empty – another positive feature of minimal formality. For lightweight paving materials, consider decking, light aggregates or composition plastic tiles. Aluminium mesh panels can provide raised walkways over awkward low walls or other partitions.

145

above left **This garden, designed by Ron Herman, is a minimalist reference to a chequerboard garden of moss and stone seen in a Zen temple in Kyoto, Japan. The precise grid is filled with rounded pebbles and fresh green helxine.**

above **A modern interior garden, like a tiny atrium, is influenced by Japanese simplicity. Water drips from a stainless steel wall plaque into a raised pool of glass bricks.**

Displaying the asymmetrical formality of Japanese gardens is this elegantly minimal courtyard, designed by Isabelle Greene. It has few plants but is animated by a river of fine grey shingle running through an earth-red gravelled 'landscape' along which lie four couchant rocks. Simply rounded clay pots and a tall coffee pot on concrete platforms act as sculptures.

opposite above *A roof garden shaded by canvas awnings is floored with timber decking. The low table with woven reed cushion seats, and the boundary trellis of fine cane, have an oriental flavour.*

opposite below *The beauty of dressed and polished rocks contrasts with the waves of coarse gravel from which they emerge, like drifting continents, in this garden of contemplation strongly influenced by the classical gardens of Japan.*

Greater exposure to the weather on a roof influences the choice of plants, even those brought out only for a summer airing. By choosing few but well-formed plants the roof garden will have its focus. Giant pampas grasses (forms of *Cortaderia*) in large deep containers would be superb because they tolerate the strongest winds. To protect from blazing summer heat, overhead canvas awnings and canopies are invaluable, for your comfort as well as the plants. But if you live in an area prone to gales, a timber or aluminium pergola, left unplanted, will filter the glare.

the Japanese effect

The irregular formality of the gardens of Kyoto in Japan is seen as an icon of modernity. The established tradition of elemental simplicity is intensely formal and has become highly influential among modern architects and designers, so well is it suited to the chic elegance of glass, concrete and steel architecture. Japanese gardens were manipulated to a fine degree, in pursuit of a philosophy of spiritual balance. Every object, living, mineral or manufactured, is appreciated for itself and for its representation of the wider landscape. The flows of nature, such as the sea or a river, are replicated as areas of precious space, randomly shaped but well textured (for example, gravel), in which a very few, perfectly maintained elements are sited. In the Buddhist garden, rules are observed and aesthetics managed with great care, always giving the appearance of effortless elegance; restraint is another leading characteristic. In the West, this has become is a garden style in itself, rather than a philosophy.

A simple, contemplative garden can be built without any living plants, choosing instead superb materials placed with great attention to detail. There may be a few crisply geometric flagstones, like travertine marble, beside grittier sandstone slabs, set in a 'sea' of gravel and backed by a plain wall of rendered concrete. The only animating feature may be water, accompanied by boulders of character grouped together or linked by eye across the void.

Gravel is much used in Japanese gardens and the minimalist garden picks up on this. In Japanese culture, raking the gravel has a symbolic role but the garden is intended only for viewing, while gravel in modern Western gardens it is nearly always walked upon as it flows like water around the site. Pavers may be set into it for comfort and to break into the area, but both materials should be the same colour. One focus set

off-centre, representing calm in the sea of space, could be a solitary plant like a multi-stemmed, 9m (30ft) high *Cercidiphyllum japonicum* with its beautiful rounded leaves, a powerfully vertical rock or a bold sculpture.

Such serenity can be interpreted without requiring an overdraft, particularly if using plants. A simple courtyard of fine shingle, its edges obscured by low clipped evergreen azaleas and its walls lined with split bamboo canes, is not costly. Or the ground may be carpeted by an expanse of mown grass, creeping evergreen *Thymus serpyllum* or deciduous *Soleirolia soleirolii*. To create elemental perfection add one still pool, set off-centre and reflecting a crouching rock.

For many people in the modern world, time has become a luxury and fewer of us have hours
to spare for the physical pleasures of gardening as a hobby. Many contemporary gardens
are therefore planned like a designed kitchen, expected to be functional and easy to run as
well as beautiful at all times of year. There is good reason to establish a permanent, formal
framework of hard landscaping and evergreen plants, but to leave gaps for more ephemeral
planting which may either reflect seasonal changes or offer the chance to alter the character
of the garden completely every year. Colour themes could be changed annually, perhaps dark
and moody one year and palely luminous the next. This is in many ways the ultimately controllable
garden, giving fast results and a reliable display. To buy new plants every year and regard
them as expendable can be an expensive way of gardening – and yet the formal, immaculate style
of many modern gardens depends on the plants being mature and looking their best at all times.

*Annual morning glory (Ipomoea
purpurea) is a rewarding summer
climber, here transforming a simple
wire pergola for one season.*

Within the permanent plant structure that establishes the formal basis on which the garden is planned, specific areas may be left unplanted for seasonal and annual effects. In a small garden, for example, the permanent framework may be no more than evergreen wall shrubs, like pyracantha and escallonia, clipped flat to line a boundary with lush greenness. Trees may be used to introduce height and provide shaded areas in an exposed garden where there would otherwise be no depths. And both evergreen and deciduous shrubs will serve to define the forms and spaces, edge routes, establish symmetry or screen the utilitarian parts of a garden. Within such a structure, the gravel or earth beds left unplanted may be filled first with spring bulbs, to be replaced when they have finished flowering by annuals or tender herbaceous perennials that appear from early spring to late autumn, to be discarded in their turn when they are over. Temporary, tender residents that are brought outdoors for the summer only would stay in their pots or containers, to be sunk below the soil or gravel bed and replaced when they are past their best. This is only possible if the garden has a small greenhouse, or the house a conservatory, where they may be stored.

annual changes

Although clipped evergreens may set an enduring framework, deciduous plants lose their foliage and gardens constantly alter. By midsummer, shrub foliage and some herbaceous flowers will often have lost their sparkle and can look tired and dusty. Planting afresh with annuals and bulbs every year ensures the garden a restorative vitality. Provided you choose those annuals that offer long-lasting flower or foliage, the garden will glow with colour for the three to four main months of summer.

For good foliage, which can add colour to the evergreen structure, consider red orach (*Atriplex hortensis*) and the silvery, half-hardy perennial grown as an annual, dusty miller (*Senecio cineraria*). For summer-long floral effects there are many annuals to choose from, like mounds of fluffy blue *Ageratum houstonianum* for rhythmical repetition, Swan River daisy (*Brachyscome iberidifolia*) planted in grid patterns and deep violet heliotropes for massed ground cover. Contrast these with tall tobacco plants (*Nicotiana*), brilliant zinnias and, for shade, the invaluable busy lizzies (*Impatiens hybrida*), particularly the white forms. As summer ends, remove and discard these annuals, replacing them with bulbs for spring.

quick effects
& permanence

seasonal infill

In this ingeniously designed garden by Victor Shanley, a grid pattern of bricks defines square paved areas. Each area holds a planting bed, edged with clipped box and holding a topiary sphere, while a line of timber cubes hold permanent topiary. By using dark yew for boundary hedging and bright green box for the inner framework, the garden is effectively the same all year round. But filling the square beds and side beds with annuals and bulbs changes its look with the seasons. In spring they are filled with white bulbs like *Tulipa* 'White Triumphator' or, as shown right, *Narcissus* 'Glacier', an elegant flower, 40cm (17in) tall, with a slim, frilled trumpet. For late-spring colour is the violet-mauve lily-flowered tulip, *T.* 'Ballade', 55cm (22in) tall with gracefully reflexed petals. One option for summer is the fragrant *Lilium x testaceum*, though its height of 1.2m (4ft) will conceal the clipped central box.

bulbous plants

The bareness of winter can have a haunting charm, with the garden more spacious-looking than at any other time. This makes it ideal for displays of bulbs and other bulbous plants that appear in spring. Bulbous plants include those that grow from bulbs, corms, tuber or rhizomes; all are forms of food storage at the base of the plant from which it will eventually grow. Where the theme is contemporarily modern, avoid planting in naturalistic clumps and plant instead in either regimented lines or massed together to create a carpet effect.

Mass planting that carpets an area has a formality of its own, reminiscent of the coloured gravels that once infilled parterres. Most bulbs are intended as permanent planting since, unlike annuals, the majority of bulbs and tubers are left in the ground from year to year. *Anemone nemorosa* 'Robinsoniana' makes a 10cm (4in) high carpet of pale blue flowers in late winter, with long-lasting ferny foliage. Like them, the slightly taller *A. blanda* series in white, blue or pink is reliably suited to shade. In a sunny spot, crocus hybrids have the same rewarding effect of covering the ground with a sheet of colour, like white *C. vernus* 'Jeanne d'Arc', purple 'Remembrance' or ivory 'Cream Delight' (all 10cm/4in high).

This carpet effect can be maintained in two ways. One is by covering the ground with shallow-rooted annual seeds, scattered directly on the soil, like massed nasturtiums (*Tropaeolum* 'Moonlight' or dark red *T. majus* 'Empress of India'), their rounded leaves trailing over the soil. Or, the mass of corms could be grown through a permanent blanket of low evergreen perennial groundcover like dwarf periwinkle (*Vinca minor*) or sweet woodruff (*Galium odoratum*), both for light shade, or massed *Helianthemum* 'Amy Baring' in full sun, so that their summer flowers provide a fresh display of colour.

For more formal, regimented effects, use tall, erect plants that can be ranked, to emphasize the lines of the garden in spring. To fulfil this role in a sunny position, tulips cannot be beaten. Look for elegant lily-flowered types like yolk-yellow *Tulipa* 'West Point', creamy-apricot 'Sapporo', 'White Triumphator' or violet 'Ballade', every petal graphically edged with white. These tulips are about 55cm (22in) tall. Strong flower colour may suit very formal or minimalist gardens, so try maroon 'Havran', almost black 'Queen of Night' or cardinal-red 'Ile de France', all a little taller. Tulips are the exception among bulbs and rarely do as well after their first year, so for immaculate effects in spring it is worth removing and discarding the bulbs after they have finished flowering and investing in new ones annually.

The startlingly formed, stately crown imperials (*Fritillaria imperialis*), 60–90cm (2–3ft) tall, have such imposing style and colour they almost belong with the exotics. Planted in well-drained soil in a sunny situation, their huge mahogany, orange or gold flowers, hanging beneath a crown rosette of spiky leaf-like bracts, grow on a single erect stem. They create dramatic and rhythmical patterns wherever they are planted.

Later in the season lilies and alliums come to the fore, both flowering in early to late summer. Lilies add fragrance and have elegant, trumpet-shaped flowers; most enjoy sunshine and well-drained soil. Lily hybrids include *Lilium* 'Casa Blanca', a heavily scented white that may grow to 1.2m (4ft), the nodding-headed Citronella Group, a spotted brilliant yellow, and the musky Pink Perfection Group, with up to 30 flowers per stem, reaching 1.5m (5ft). All rivet attention when they are in flower. For shaded areas look for the recurved 'turk's cap' type of lily, the soft purple-brown *L. martagon* and *L. martagon* var. *album*, both 1–2m (3ft 3in–6ft 6in) tall. These will spread over the years but are far more modest in appearance than the hybrids described above.

Alliums have such a strong shape that they suit the formal garden well. The huge *A. giganteum* is a drumstick of 1.2m (4ft) with hundreds of tiny lilac-coloured flowers forming a perfectly rounded globe atop a single stem. In full sun these alliums can present regimented lines along a path or flanking a pergola walk. The smaller *A. cristophii*, 60cm (2ft) tall, has larger globes. Unlike tulips that tend to deteriorate, alliums will increase in numbers year after year.

151

The tapering box-edged parterre is filled with permanent domes of clipped box, but room is left for a mixture of red with pink and white tulips to bring colour in spring.

annuals, biennials and tender perennials

Annuals have a short but very sweet life, needing to display and make seed in one season – and what a display it can be. In weed-free cultivated soil, raked to a fine tilth, you can plant hardy annual seeds – like clarkia, nemophila, mallow and love-in-a-mist (*Nigella*) – where they are to grow and watch the gradual greening over of the soil. The seeds of biennials need time to germinate, so they are sown a year ahead, taking two years to flower, like *Salvia sclarea* or Icelandic poppies (*Papaver nudicaule*). Or you can plant out, after the last frost, tender annuals and biennials raised by you, or a nursery, under cover in the preceding autumn or spring.

An alternative to time-consuming sowing and transplanting is to buy plugs or polystyrene starter packs of pre-prepared bedding, ready for planting out in spring. The choice will be limited but success more likely: plant them close together to conceal bare soil. Be aware of your local climatic conditions so that where late frost is a possibility you do not plant tender annuals too early. Read the instructions on the packet, as requirements differ.

To start the season, the biennial white honesty (*Lunaria annua* 'Alba Variegata'), planted the previous autumn, may be massed in light shade and annuals such as cosmos can continue from summer to autumn in sun. French marigolds will provide brilliant textures at ground level. The mahogany-striped *Tagetes* 'Mr Majestic' or rust-red *T. patula* 'Cinnabar' are 30cm (12in) tall and fill sunny ground like lush rugs. The old biennial sweet williams have a cooler effect and are taller, like *Dianthus barbatus*

summer colour and texture

Galvanized steel containers hold evergreen black bamboo (*Phyllostachys nigra*) all year round, but you can ring the changes each summer in the bed set into wooden decking at their foot. Here, pretty perennial Iceland poppies (*Papaver nudicaule*) provide delicate summer colour and are well suited to the slate mulch. For different effects, use annuals which revel in hot sunlight. For a splash of colour, choose a delicate clump of scarlet flax (*Linum rubrum*, below left) or the more showy, mat-forming gazanias (*Gazania* 'Talent', centre) with their bright daisy flowers. Both suit a hot, dry position and flower in the height of midsummer. A more subtle candidate would be the tuft-forming annual hare's-tail grass (*Lagurus ovatus* 'Bunny Tails', right), whose fluffy cream flowers last into autumn.

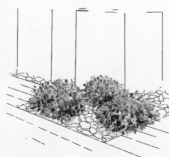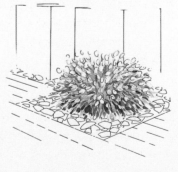

'Indian Carpet', in mixed pink and white, and the velvety chocolate-red *D. barbatus* 'Sooty'.

Even tall, architecturally shaped annuals can be grown in one season, like huge sunflowers (*Helianthus*) in sun and foxgloves (*Digitalis*) in light shade. Spectacular cultivars of *Helianthus* are now available in diverse heights, flower size, texture and colour. Pale cream *H.* 'White Delight' has a single cream flower at 1.5m (5ft), 'Velvet Queen' is darkly Venetian red and the same height, and *H. annuus* 'Sunspot' has yellow flowers 60cm (2ft) in diameter. There are double-flowered and branched forms too, but for modern gardens the simpler shapes are the best. Along a white wall in the minimal garden they would be both cheerful and dramatic.

The old-fashioned single hollyhock (*Alcea rosea*) makes spikes that may reach 2m (6ft 6in) in mid- to late summer in sun. The drawback is that their rounded lobed leaves attract rust, which can spoil the pristine effects of a formal garden. Rank hollyhocks beside a heavy timber fence or grow them as a group with rounded rocks for a focal effect. The white foxglove (*Digitalis purpurea* f. *albiflora*) is a perennial best grown as a biennial, with new ones planted every year. They add a soft effect in a garden of minimalist perfection.

Since abstinence is the new *cause célèbre* of once plant-hungry gardeners, planting may be spare but beautiful in the minimalist gravelled garden. So annual Californian or opium poppies – *Eschscholzia californica*, with a 30cm (12in) tall flower, and *Papaver somniferum* at 75cm (2ft 6in) – are ideal for early flowering and successful seeding that can be 'edited out' as required, to leave a balance of plant vitality with clear open space. For a garden where colour is minimally reduced to shades of white, a 60cm (2ft) high ground spread of *Arctotis fastuosa* 'Zulu Prince' could be grown as an annual in a hot gravelled space, or *Cosmos bipinnatus* 'Sonata White' would be softer, having feathery moss-green foliage.

Many tender perennials originating in hot countries can be grown as annuals in temperate climates. Some salvias have exquisitely subtle flowers in luminous purples and blues. *Salvia farinacea* 'Victoria' produces spikes of deep purple flowers carried to a height of 45cm (18in) and *S. sclarea* var. *turkestanica* is spectacularly pink, white and powder-blue, right through to early autumn, looking wonderful with polished steel, reflective glass or translucent polycarbonate walls and screens.

Dark-coloured plants suit contemporary gardens. Here, a shrubby perennial purple osier (Salix purpurea 'Gracilis') offers pewtered, dark purple leaf colour alongside two Acer palmatum 'Versicolor'. Both rise above clumps of blue Festuca glauca, but it is the summer planting of red impatiens that enriches the colour associations.

exotic and sculptural specimens

As climatic changes seem to be under way, choosing to use tender 'exotics' becomes an exciting possibility. 'Exotic' of course depends upon your viewpoint; cow parsley would be exotic in Arizona. But the word is generally taken to encompass strikingly shaped, huge-leaved plants, often from sub-tropical climates (exotic and architecturally shaped plants are discussed more fully in Part 1). They look great in a modern, cleanly formal setting with a plain background and uncomplicated flooring.

Different effects can be created, for example using the frost-hardy fan palm (see page 73) to set the skeletal form of a large garden scheme in lines, like an avenue. The half-hardy dwarf fan palm can be used on a smaller scale to mark directions or as an evergreen part of a dramatic year-round group. Pure theatre may appeal for one summer, using tall, dramatic attention-seekers to add panache to formal beds. Choose the biennial *Echium wildpretii*, a columnar spectacle of 2m (6ft 6in), or the strange, pewter-grey annual larkspur (*Consolida ajacis* 'Earl Grey') that grows to 1.2m (4ft). Both can be grown in containers as annuals. Many annuals offer strikingly different textural effects to offset these prima donnas, like the annual grass *Hordeum jubatum* (60cm/2ft) or the furry lamb's-tail flowers of *Amaranthus* 'Hopi Red Dye'.

permanent planting

If there is but one living thing in a minimalist courtyard, it should have year-round architectural form, but if it is also an exotic it will conjure up images of distant places and different climates. Consider the oriental effect of the yellow canes and bright green foliage of the 4m (13ft) tall bamboo *Phyllostachys aureosulcata* 'Spectabilis'. This is ideal permanently planted in an isolated position; if really well suited, it may reach its natural height of 8m (27ft). A Japanese acer, like *Acer palmatum* 'Chitoseyama' would suggest an oriental exoticism, with skeletal elegance in winter. Other drama queens include the knife-sharp spears of yuccas, cordylines and phormiums (see page 73), all evergreen. These are plants with style and character that, grown alone, will replace sculpture as the aesthetic focus of a modern formal garden. By contrast, the softer, sword-like perennials like crocosmias, irises and astelia are less dominant, so better used in quantity.

temporary planting

Other large-foliaged exotics are more exciting if planted together. Planned ahead, but planted in late spring, after the last frost, a large group arising from a bed cut into immaculately bonded fine gravel would dominate in summer. They could include the palmate-leaved, half-hardy shrub *Ricinus communis*: look for 'Impala', a form with dark bronze-red foliage. Cannas look wonderful in association, so consider variegated *Canna malawiensis* 'Variegata' or staunch *C. iridiflora*, a form with rich orange flowers.

Dahlias fit well with such opulent planting: *Dahlia* 'Bishop of Llandaff' is a single-flowered, rich red which will survive outside in winter. But most dahlias should be lifted and possibly stored, like the cannas and ricinus. The anemone-flowered *D.* 'Comet' and a pompon, *D.* 'Whale's Rhonda', are equally intensely red. Cactus-flowered types look incredibly exotic, as there is nothing in temperate planting quite as flamboyantly structured: look for the appropriately named orange *D.* 'Quel Diable'. In a group, they have enormous presence in the garden, making sculpture redundant.

Patience has always been one of the strictures applied to gardening, but of all the advantages gardeners have today the possibility of buying maturity is one of the most useful. This is costly but effective. Show gardens, for example, can be set up within a week, using huge plants in huge containers, and if your garden is minimally planned it may be worth the expense of buying in a few mature specimens. Be sure, however, that you have room for the very large rootballs that come with them and note the importance of well-prepared soil for planting and regular watering for the first year. Even in winter, do not allow large specimens to dry out and occasionally check that the wind has not rocked them, tearing the new fine roots as they try to establish the large plant in its permanent home.

Towards the end of summer dahlias inflame the garden with colour. Here they are massed together to edge a pebble path leading to a tranquil pool encircled by a frame of woven willow.

exotic effects

Shiny industrial drums of galvanized steel make exciting containers for tomatoes in a contemporary kitchen garden. The spiralling effect of the steel strips has a celebratory air, like flags at Agincourt, while the shallow water in which they stand ensures damp soil. For a more ornamental look, exotic plants make ideal subjects, with strong form and colours. The cabbage palm (*Cordyline australis* 'Albertii') is a dominating plant with leafy, strap-shaped swords; contained, its height is restricted to 2m (6ft 6in). The perennial castor oil plant (*Ricinus communis*) also looks exotic, with palmate foliage. Vulnerable to frost, it is often grown as an annual; it reaches 1m (3ft 3in) in a summer. Perennial cannas have long been planted as annuals: *Canna iridiflora* 'Ehemannii', from Peru, grows to 2m (6ft), with long, paddle-shaped leaves and waxy red flower panicles in high summer.

using containers

In the modern formal context containers may be built in as part of a concrete fitted garden, in the form of troughs large enough for shrubs. Or large, freestanding containers can be regarded as permanent features, part of the linear design if they are placed to emphasize lines, to mark a crossing or changed direction. (Containers as sculpture is discussed in Part 1, page 55.) These are often most appropriately repeat-planted with identical specimens of the same height and maturity – like tulips or lilies, clipped box domes or clumps of dwarf bamboo. Some containers are chosen to be mobile and can be shifted around the garden as plants come into their own, then retired to a quieter area until they are beautiful